THE 100 TRILLION DOLLAR WEALTH TRANSFER

THE 100 TRILLION DOLLAR WEALTH TRANSFER

How the Handover from Boomers to Gen Z Will Revolutionize Capitalism

KEN COSTA

BLOOMSBURY CONTINUUM
LONDON • OXFORD • NEW YORK • NEW DELHI • SYDNEY

BLOOMSBURY CONTINUUM
Bloomsbury Publishing Plc
50 Bedford Square, London, WC1B 3DP, UK
29 Earlsfort Terrace, Dublin 2, Ireland

BLOOMSBURY, BLOOMSBURY CONTINUUM and the Diana logo are trademarks
of Bloomsbury Publishing Plc

First published in Great Britain 2023

A catalogue record for this book is available from the British Library

Library of Congress Cataloguing-in-Publication data has been applied for

ISBN: HB: 978-1-3994-0763-2; TPB: 978-1-3994-1250-6; eBook: 978-1-3994-0764-9;
ePDF: 978-1-3994-0768-7

2 4 6 8 10 9 7 5 3 1

Typeset by Deanta Global Publishing Services, Chennai, India
Printed and bound in Great Britain by CPI Group (UK) Ltd, Croydon CR0 4YY

To find out more about our authors and books visit www.bloomsbury.com
and sign up for our newsletters

CONTENTS

ACKNOWLEDGEMENTS

This book has been in gestation for over a decade. After the Global Financial Crisis, I delivered a series of lectures as the Gresham Professor of Commerce in Gresham College, London. Many of the key thoughts in this book have their origin in those lectures, which explored how capitalism had slipped its moral moorings and how the destruction of trust in the market economy would impact the next generation. I am grateful to Gresham College for the opportunity to reflect on these issues at such a pivotal time.

I have had the privilege of mentoring, coaching, investing and socialising with a wide range of Zennials in the UK, USA, South Africa, Hong Kong, Singapore and Australia. They are the anonymous contributors to the book, as are my friends and colleagues in the financial world. I hope they will recognise, albeit without attribution, some of the thoughts that appear in the book.

The teams at Midas and Bloomsbury, and Tomasz Hoskins in particular, have been unwavering in their encouragement throughout the writing process and working to ensure that the vital themes covered in the book reach the right audience. I would also like to thank Rory Marsden, Daniel Kim and Matthew Richardson for their help in researching and drawing out the key themes reflected in the book, as well as the unstinting help and contribution of my Executive Assistant, Lexi Jackson.

I am particularly thankful for the many conversations, criticism and manuscript reading by my family: Georgina, Nicholas, Charles, Henry, Jenny, Claudia and Ben. I am so proud of their challenging and rigorous comments. I am forever grateful to my patient wife, Fi who has had to put up with a constant stream of new ideas at various times of day and night. She has been both encouraging of the project and helpfully dismissive of my sometimes wayward ideas.

Finally, I'd like to thank those Zennials and Boomers who are already using CO to work together and trusting each other to find the crucial solutions to the problems our planet faces, and which can only be solved by collaboration across the generations.

INTRODUCTION

A major shift is occurring. You may not have felt it yet. But you will. Money, power and influence are on the move. Assets worth 100 trillion dollars are shifting from one generation to the next. The shift has started already. It's imperceptible to most observers. But in the US alone, $84 trillion of assets will transfer from older generations – predominantly mine, the so-called baby boomers, all of whom will be at least 65 by 2030 – to our children in the Millennial and Zoomer generations.[1] In the UK, the corresponding figure is estimated at £5.5 trillion.[2] This is the largest flow of generational capital ever seen in the history of humanity. This is the Great Wealth Transfer of our age. And how we deal with this legacy will change the way we live now and reshape the global economy.

Because a new generation, who are committed to the emerging of a new form of capitalism – socially energized capitalism – is beginning to take hold of the levers of change. They are receiving and will inherit capital from parents and grandparents. And this flow of capital is already underway. In the UK, the so-called Bank of Mum and Dad is providing the capital for this generation to get themselves on the property ladder. They are becoming hugely financially empowered. And, meanwhile, technology has empowered this generation as never before to make an impact. Their influence and voice are being heard at all levels of the economy and society and their numbers are growing worldwide. The impact they will make is huge, because how they decide to move the levers of change and use their newfound capital either destroys capitalism or saves it. That's the reality. This is a major tectonic shift in capitalism. It has already started in earnest and will only gain pace over the coming decades as huge amounts of wealth continue to move between generations with very different principles and outlook. We live in an age of inheritocracy.[3]

Driven by this new empowered generation, the social, political and financial tectonic plates of our world are moving. Tectonic shifts are what have built the world as we know it. They're the reason we live on multiple different continental blocks rather than one supercontinent, where a gentle stroll from San Francisco to Tokyo would be a possibility. They're the reason the Himalayas exist, and continue to grow higher and higher every year. They're also responsible for the Pacific Ring of Fire, the 25,000-mile string of 452 volcanoes that stretches from the southern tip of South America, up along the coast of North America, across the Bering Strait, down through Japan, and into New Zealand.

But I'm not a geologist. I'm not here to tell you about the formation of a new continent. Or the rising of the Himalayas Mark II. I am, though, talking about a shift of similar significance to humankind and society as we know it.

Four drivers will shape this future: the generational shift in wealth; the consequent empowerment of the next generation to implement their social and political objectives; the power of influence driven by the exponential growth in technology; and the youthening of the global population. As never before in history, these drivers will be weaponized to achieve the mission of these coming-of-age, activist, agents of change.

THE SHIFT FROM BOOMERS TO ZOOMERS

The major shift that will make or break the future of the market economy is intergenerational. It is not just huge amounts of money that are on the move to the younger generations. Power is as well. By 2030, Millennials alone will make up 75 per cent of the global workforce. Just by pure weight of numbers, they will be the ones, along with their Gen Z successors, whose opinions matter most. The two groups (who I will refer to together as Zennials) are remarkably similar. They are tech-savvy – and crucially tech-empowered – digital natives who, broadly speaking, distrust the economic, social and political systems that were responsible for, most significantly, 2008's Global Financial Crisis (GFC). It will be their principles that guide the business plans of the future. Indeed, they are already guiding the business plans of today. Boardrooms worldwide are well aware of the need to be relevant for this socially conscious and digitally reliant generation, who are sceptics of the market economy and will not become passive participants as the previous generation were.

Zennial representatives will walk the halls of power across the globe over the coming decades; indeed, some of them already have, or are already there. Chilean president Gabriel Boric is 37, as is Finland's former Prime Minister Sanna Marin. By some definitions, former New Zealand Prime Minister Jacinda Ardern (born in 1980) is a Millennial.

In short, while Boomer money will have a huge part to play in bankrolling the future, their influence is on the way out. And their children have very different ideas on how they want the world to run. We are entering the Zennial age. They will have the power, not least through technology but also through the capital they are inheriting, to throw out the past and implement the future they want. It will be an age in which a socially energized generation has the financial muscle and technological resources to bend capitalism to its will, to the point that it either breaks or moves. They want to shape, not be shaped, by the world they have been handed. They live to change the world, to rebuild it in their own image. It's a purposeful mission, not merely a passing meme. The presuppositions of a previous generation will matter little.

Herein lie the seeds of danger. Not all of the past needs to be dismissed as being destructive, and not all of the future aspirations of Zennials are to be desired. Notwithstanding the power of this Zennial wave, the Boomer generation still has a key corrective contribution to make.

In 2020, Charlotte Alter wrote in *Time* magazine that '[Millennial] startups have revolutionized the economy, their tastes have shifted the culture, and their enormous appetite for social media has transformed human interaction. American politics is the next arena ripe for disruption.' But it's bigger than that even. The inheritance of capital, power and influence by Zennials is going to change everything. Technology will be their tool, a tool more effective than any newly empowered generation has had previously, so the rate of change will be rapid. We need to be prepared. Because these changes will lead either to the destruction of our way of life as we know it or to the necessary building of a new, better capitalism.

The intergenerational shift is the biggest shift set to take place in the coming decades. But it is not the only one of significance to capitalism globally, although it will inform other moves set to take place.

GO EAST

Anyone even vaguely paying attention since the turn of the millennium will know that the world's economic centre of gravity has been on the move for two decades. That's certainly what Allianz, one of the world's leading financial institutions, has established.[4] The West is hardly deteriorating as a major financial power. But it is slowly ceding ground to the East when it comes to being the biggest players in the global economy. Additionally, relative economic recovery speeds in the wake of the Covid-19 pandemic have only served to steepen the curve.

In 2000, developed economies represented around 80 per cent of global GDP. That ratio fell to around 60 per cent in 2019, with the Asia-Pacific region responsible for 8 of the 20 percentage points.[5] In actual geographic terms, Allianz has found that the world's economic centre of gravity between 1998 to 2019 has moved from the North Atlantic Ocean – not far from the United States' east coast – to the Middle East. And the direction of travel is only going one way. By 2030, that centre of gravity 'could be located around the confluence of China, India and Pakistan'.

This shift is being driven by Zennials in this part of the world. A global youthening, as it were. In 2014, the United Nations Population Fund reported that India had the world's highest number of 10- to 24-year-olds, with 356 million, ahead of China, with 269 million, Indonesia with 67 million, the United States with 65 million, and Pakistan with 59 million.[6] The youngest of these young people are now nearing their twenties, the oldest deep into their thirties, and they want to shape the future of their societies.

GREEN IS GOOD

Decarbonizing the energy system is an existential necessity. A fundamental transformation in the way we provide, transport and consume energy is required, which means a major shift from brown energy – fossil fuels like oil, coal and gas – to green energy. Be in no doubt at all that this shift will have a major impact on our capitalism. It has been calculated that global supply chains need $100 trillion of investment by 2050 if they're to achieve net zero, with as much as half of that required by small and medium-sized enterprises.[7]

The overall impact of policies to move towards net zero emissions is expected to be largely positive from an economic perspective.[8] But in the process some sectors will benefit while others, most obviously oil and gas extraction, will decline. The shift in capital required to achieve net zero is staggering and it will impact on every corner of the global economy, chiefly because Zennials will refuse to allow this transformation not to happen. They will use their newfound power, influence and financial muscle to ensure it does. And they will have no qualms about tearing down established institutions in their bid to achieve this goal. Again, this will have enormous real-world implications when it comes to capital, and how and where it is apportioned. Boomers and Zennials will agree on these objectives but will struggle over how the changes will be paid for. Capitalism is at risk if the strident Zennial call for greater taxation is not tempered by the Boomer experience of the need for wealth to be created before it can be distributed, however urgent the cause may be.

THE FEMINIZATION OF FINANCE

The final obvious shift set to occur over the coming decades is the gender-split in who controls the world's capital. This shift is happening rapidly and has similar implications for global capitalism as those listed above because it will require a similar adaptation, if not reconstruction, of the status quo. We will fundamentally have to change the way we think about money: how, where and why it is spent.

In the US, for example, women currently control and manage around $10 trillion in financial assets. That figure is expected to reach $30 trillion by the end of the current decade.[9]

It is McKinsey analysis that has established these figures, and their report[10] advises that 'attracting and retaining female customers will be a critical growth imperative for wealth management firms. To succeed, firms will need to deeply understand women's differentiated needs, preferences, and behaviours when it comes to managing their money.' And most of these women will be Zennials. So, in short, it will be a 'critical growth imperative' to understand Zennial needs, preferences and behaviours.

This idea can be applied to all four of the above shifts I have mentioned and is something that our society as a whole needs to take on board if capitalism as we know it is to survive into the next century. This is not just social observation. Not just theoretical. Every workplace across the globe will be impacted by the shifts that are occurring within capitalism as you read this. Business as usual is coming to an end. Something new is forming, and it will reflect Zennial objectives. We need to respond. Deep understanding is exactly what is required and it is the intention of this book to provide a path to it.

BREAKING OUT OF THE SILOS

Identity is the key social issue of our time. Social media fuels a desire to divide into tribes and then attack other tribes with all the intensity of religious conflict. A collective sense of belonging means that there is no need for dispassionate thinking. Just choose the tribe and don't worry, the brand will carry your convictions. The crisis is that, once a tribe is chosen the whole agenda has to be accepted. The pernicious effect is that becoming part of the silo removes the ability to pick and choose. There is a need for both Zennials and Boomers (whose tribes are as rigid but perhaps not digitally fuelled) to work towards breaking down these barriers of misunderstanding and anger.

Because the shifts that are occurring are creating cracks. Fault lines are everywhere. Divisions abound. As we near the end of the twenty-first century's Quarter 1, the first 25 years, it seems our fields of vision are consistently narrowing. It has not, thus far, been a century of tolerance, unity and open-mindedness. Or even just optimism. It's been a century in which we have retreated into silos, cut ourselves off. The 'echo chamber' effect. Cynicism is in. Tribalism is in. The no-man's-land between right and left on the political spectrum seems to widen by the day. As does the chasm between the haves and the have-nots, the powerful and the powerless.

Unfortunately, generational conflicts are particularly keen. The older generations patronize their children, who rage at their elders for the mess they've left them in. It's not a pretty picture. A world of factions convinced that they are right and everybody else is wrong. That they've nothing to learn from an opposing view, nor anything to share. And everything is designed to ossify that position; the newspapers we read tell us what we want to hear, the tech we use leads us deeper into entrenchment. Even where we choose to live divides us. Unlike in previous centuries, young and old are now separated by geography as the former move to cities and the latter leave them. Young people and old people used to live, work and socialize alongside each other wherever they were. As recently as 1991 in the UK, villages and cities had the same mix of ages.[11] Now, though, that is no longer the case. The median age of the population of the UK in 2020 was just over 40.[12] But the average age of a Londoner was 35. This has a major impact because it means a breakdown in dialogue between generations. As *The Times*'s James Marriott has pointed out: 'Think of almost any party in any novel written in the 19th century: the young dance with each other while watched over by their elders sitting around the edge of the room.'[13] Generations used to interact with each other in all walks of life. Now they don't. That is a problem.

Throughout my career in finance we have had 'town hall' gatherings to bring together the people in a company and to help build a camaraderie through communicating well, while aligning the executives with the aspirations of the business. The effects have been a drawing together and, hopefully, bonding through transparency, consultation and socializing. The digital version of this gathering achieves the opposite. It fuels division and rancour. It produces self-righteous commentary in rapid-fire rather than reflective form. Its format is often a Twitter rage with inflammatory short words: pissed off, hypocrite, disgusting, etc.

SOCIALLY ENERGIZED CAPITALISM

We cannot continue down this road and deal effectively with the society-altering shifts we are about to encounter. It's one or the other. Adapt or die, you might say. We must break out of our silos and find common ground. Because there are two roads before us: a narrow one, leading us to a more inclusive, purposeful capitalism that still incentivizes good business; and a wide one, leading to a bitter ideological conflict that poses a threat to the hard-won stability of the global economy, driven by intergenerational tensions. Failure to adapt capitalism in line with the shifts that are occurring will result in its destruction.

So what's the answer? Partially, it's the socially energized capitalism I talked of before, the lifeblood of the new Zennial capitalism. A capitalism that is defined not exclusively by a desire to make money but that incorporates the objectives of a socially conscious generation who have a desire for real change. Breaking down these silos will be a cooperative effort, requiring intentionality, reasoned argument, humility, unpretentious honouring of different views and the avoidance of sloganeering.

HAVE FAITH IN ZENNIALS

If typical representations of Zennials are anything to go by, the coming shift – in which they effectively inherit the earth – is one we should all be deathly afraid of, right? Because surely Zennials – this lazy, entitled, self-obsessed, materialistic cohort – do not have what it takes to handle such huge responsibility? They don't have the right work ethic. They'll just spend all the money on smashed avocado and therapy. And then where will we be?

I'd like, here, to present the opposite view. That, in fact, the Zennial generation are brilliantly suited for this responsibility exactly because they are so different from their parents. Nowhere is this more obvious than in the differing proprietary instincts of the two generations. My Boomer contemporaries and I have defined our lives through what we own. It has been our mark of progress; whether it be owning a car, a house, a business. Proprietary involvement has been the key defining piece of the postwar generation: owning and building assets. It was always seen as the best possible investment globally.

But this has changed. Yes, it has been partially enforced because younger generations simply have not been able to afford to be asset rich. But as a result they have come to appreciate the economic advantage in being asset light, as well as the social advantages of shared ownership.

Zennials in 2023 – or certainly those I know, my children and their friends – scoff at the idea of insuring one's car all year round; how pointless given that you can now buy insurance trip to trip and save money as a result. Indeed, why own a car at all when the likes of Zipcar remove the burden of responsibility while having little impact on convenience? And again, in this example, the social and environmental instincts of this generation come to the fore. Zennials essentially are prepared to give up ownership because they are motivated by the fact they're capable of sharing a scarce resource. There is no need for everyone, certainly in a major city, to own a car, so why not share one?

There has been a noticeable and conscious move away from single ownership towards shared ownership. Zennials who have been excluded from the former have started to question whether they even want to own at all, given ownership is no longer a measure of success or aspiration, and now that it is so simple to share thanks to technology, whether it be a cab (Uber), office space (WeWork) or your own home (Airbnb).

This Zennial attitude towards ownership, this loss of the proprietary instinct if you like, will inform the socially energized capitalism of the coming decades. Interestingly, it was a view typified by my first employer, Sir Siegmund Warburg (1902–1982), widely regarded as perhaps the greatest banker of his generation. He, much like Zennials, believed in milking assets for all they are worth but believed multiple assets were an encumbrance. This is the attitude that will now prevail among the generation set to inherit the earth.

There is no doubt we face a challenging future, but it is one I am excited by and wish to explore; because I genuinely believe there is a way we can come out the other side refreshed and improved. However, there is also danger ahead. There couldn't not be, given the shifts that are taking place. There is a reciprocity required here, as both sides of the generational divide need to come together to form a learning community, both need to recognize the need to break down silos and appreciate the contributions of both Boomers and Zennials.

INTRODUCING CO

If these shifts are not responded to deftly and effectively, we could be looking at an extinction-level event for capitalism. Because Zennials' demands will be heard and progressively they will deploy capital and influence to ensure this. They want to disrupt industries, create new environments and implement major changes in places of work the world over. They are not happy to put up with our current capitalism, which is outdated and ill-equipped for the coming decades.

What I'm talking about is the culture that was established in the formative years of my professional life, the 1980s. The me-first world. The loads-a-money caricature. The Gordon-Gekko-Greed-is-Good culture. Michael Lewis in his 1989 book *Liar's Poker* – one of the definitive books about Wall Street in the 1980s – wrote that 'the place was governed by the simple understanding that the unbridled pursuit of perceived self-interest was healthy'. He was referring specifically to Salomon Brothers, the investment bank at which he worked. But it is a fairly accurate summation of the attitude that has underpinned capitalism up until now. That culture, though, has had its day. Those who are set to assume power – in all walks of life – over the coming decades will not accept this. And this is where the key tension lies, between the attitudes of those passing on the capital, and those receiving it.

Those who have come of age in the years after the Global Financial Crisis of 2008 want a new type of capitalism, a new way of working, a new ethos that will pervade and underpin every part of the market economy. And I believe we need to embrace this if we are to avoid catastrophe. The recent failure of Silicon Valley Bank has further fuelled the level of distrust in the banking system as its effects have massively impacted Zennial entrepreneurs, start-ups and tech businesses. Yet again the governments have had to bail out a bank. And the generational distrust grows as if no lessons were learned in the GFC. A new way of working is needed. This new way of working is what I call CO.

In essence, CO is a shift from the radical individualism of post-war generations, to a prioritization of collaboration, compassion, community and collective experience. More succinctly, it's a shift from *me* to *we*. A shift to understanding that what individuals can gain from working together in CO is greater than what they give up in order to participate. We give up far less than we gain by acting together. And the gains are economic as well as ethical.

These key principles are underpinned not by self-interest, as in the past, but by collaboration and the knowledge that it is an absolute necessity to avoid tribalism or else the greed-is-good model could return and destroy us. It is necessary, therefore, to begin with the idea that everyone works together and that everyone has something to offer. From an intergenerational perspective, this means understanding that young and old, Zennials and Boomers, can contribute in the new capitalism; the former with their *insight*, energy and desire to be change-agents, the latter with their *hindsight*, their wisdom and their desire to know the world is in good hands. Together these create the *foresight* needed to steward the scarce resources of the planet and change the way we live and work together. Because I am sure Zennials don't want to do away with capitalism. They may be after socially energized capital, but that still exists within capitalism. And Zennials will need Boomer experience as a corrective to ensure they don't steer the new capitalism down the wrong path.

Crucially, CO is *not* socialism. CO is not surrendering our businesses or projects to a centralized state, nor is it the dismantling of the individual dream. Instead, it is a belief that individual dreams really can work together for the benefit of everyone. It is a commitment to the notion that the economy need not be a zero-sum game. It is a desire not simply to 'collaborate', but to truly do things as co-equals. To co-own property and ideas; co-lead ventures and startups; co-work in shared spaces; co-exist in society with all its diversity; and build a co-destiny that determines the shape of our future together on this planet. There is an ongoing push to include as many people as possible in decisions; a desire to do things together. It is the move from *I Phone* to *We Work*. And CO-inspired language is everywhere.

Co-working, co-leading, co-owning, co-creating, co-investing, co-founding are all recognizable concepts. I've even heard talk of co-determination for the new global politic, and 'co-belligerence' when in modern-day activism. I believe that this is not simply a marketing trend but an emergent force for good that has implications for our communities, leaders, religions and economies. Traditional forms of leadership are changing: the idea of a single 'great man' leading a movement is being replaced by a network of co-leaders mustering an organization. From 'Take me to your leader' to 'Take me to your network.'

In the economic space, CO means that the duty and desire for capital growth should co-exist with the duty and desire to do good by the planet and its people. CO can help us towards a level of global cooperation that will result in the environmental change necessary to save the planet and reduce CO_2. The self-interest that previously dominated is replaced with co-interest. Doing well and doing good are co-equal considerations in the Zennials' new vision of capitalism. The Zennials are set on deploying capital in a way that harmonizes capital value, with ethical values, taking into account the impact on the collective.

For us Boomers, ethical values were aspirations but pure capital value was always the imperative. Cut costs, increase profits, dial down empathy and plead ignorance. Zennials, however, cannot imagine a world in which you can have value without values. We used to say, 'run a profitable business and make it purposeful'. Today, it's 'run a purposeful business and make a profit'. The trillions of dollars flowing behind these idealistic aspirations will be like an avalanche of socially energized capital changing the face of capitalism.

I believe these Zennials to be a prophetic generation. They show deep insight into care for the environment, equality and social justice. These are not appendages to the economic ecosystem or nice-to-haves but are now front and centre. Many decry this as a failed generational shift. It is not. It is changing the way we live, think and share in the digital world. Zennials are raising fundamental questions about what it is to be human in a dehumanized society, where disruptive technology has been allowed to reign supreme, and where moral virtues have fallen asleep at the wheel. I believe Zennials are not just another demographic marked by calendar dates like the 'roaring-Twenties' or the 'swinging-Sixties', but are ushering in a new era for capitalism. A great compassionate disruption is underway and it will become the mainstream. It will become ingrained in the new way of rewiring businesses for the digital age.

The shift will not be without incident but it must be navigated effectively if capitalism is still to exist when we come out the other side. The way that we steer our way through is, appropriately, by working together. Because the hindsight of what might be termed as the 'old guard' – me and my contemporaries – will be incredibly valuable in achieving CO. Indeed, CO cannot be achieved purely through the insight of those who are spearheading it. The experience, wisdom, corrective interventions and warnings of those who have lived through capitalism in its previous form will be invaluable, particularly when the CO pendulum swings erratically or ideologically too far one way. Indeed, in terms of the crucial type of sight required for CO to succeed, foresight is the real silver bullet. It is through a combination of Zennial insight and Boomer hindsight that we can earn our collective foresight.

We are at a pivotal point in the emergence of a new way in which capital is earned, invested and deployed. CO is the method through which we can work together to move forward, rather than Zennials' values being forcibly imposed on the world. If the Boomers and Zennials explore this together, we might cooperatively implement this new season of capitalism with compassion and wisdom.

WHY ME?

You may be asking yourself what qualifies me to make such an assessment about the future of capitalism, and also what qualifies me to suggest a possible way forward. I have spent a near half-century career in finance, and have worked with both the old school and new school of capitalism. I am, undoubtedly, a product of the 1980s financial world. And, of course, I am a Boomer. But I understand the aspirations and motivations of the Zennial generation, having worked closely with many of them in the latter part of my career: investing in them, coaching them, mentoring them, advising them, and yes, when needed, correcting and chastening harmful ideological extremes.

I am not an economist but a financier with an acute and privileged knowledge of the next generation. I have a firm belief that we have an opportunity, indeed an obligation, to improve our capitalism over the coming decade. But it can only be achieved if the old school and the new school learn to work together, to collaborate. This is not something that comes naturally at present. There is often antipathy between the two generations. But I believe a fresh perspective of capitalism is coming into the mainstream of economics.

As an illustration, I recently visited a family in Italy who own a major industrial company worth several billion dollars. The key issue that the Zennial inheritor wanted to discuss was not the prospects of the company itself – which was doing very well and likely to continue doing so – but how the company could utilize its resources and capital to achieve educational objectives. What was significant about this was that in our generation this would almost certainly have been set up in a charitable foundation separate from the organization. But he was insistent that this objective was embedded in the very DNA of the company, despite the fact that the company is a basic industrial company with no educational operations. Without this commitment, he believed they would not be able to bring about the social change that the company, with its significant resources, infrastructure and capital, could do. They needed the company's muscle to promote community-based educational objectives. An example of socially energized capitalism in action. I believe this model will continue.

As I write this, 'goblin mode' has just been announced as the Oxford word of the year for 2022, a term that describes 'unapologetically self-indulgent, lazy, slovenly, or greedy' behaviour.[14] Or as many of my generation would see it, typical Zennial behaviour. Meanwhile, there will be many Zennials who would mercilessly ridicule any Boomer that attempted to use the term in conversation. This is a fairly facile example but it does illustrate the cultural rift that has opened up between the two cohorts. It is essential this becomes a thing of the past.

So over the course of this book my aim is to explain the predicament at hand and the obstacles we face as a society, and then outline the way in which I believe we can overcome them. The fundamental question is: how will the next generation better reshape the future of capitalism and society as a whole? Because reshape and transform it they will. And it will either be terrible or incredible. We need to ensure it's the latter.

I make one appeal before we dive in. In trying to draw a picture of the generations I have used the binocular method. I have drawn together two contrasting demographic groups – Boomer and Zennial – in order to compare and contrast their contributions, bringing together these two perspectives into one shape and with a sharper focus. As with binoculars, the distance set can be in clear focus, sharp and magnified, while the space in between is blurred. This will inevitably lead to some generational generalizations. I have kept these to maintain a sharp focus rather than qualifying every statement, and leading to what the philosopher Antony Flew described as a proposition dying the death of a thousand qualifications. The binoculars are meant to synthesize both perspectives, the Boomer and the Zennial, I hope to the satisfaction of my reader.

I

The Generation Game

In a recent survey, one in five executive leaders agreed with the statement: 'No one wants to work.'[1] This is not a new complaint, particularly from older generations towards the youth of whatever day they are in.

'It is becoming apparent that nobody wants to work these hard times', complained a letter to the *Rooks County Record* in Kansas in 1894. Eleven years later, another letter, this time to the *Edgefield Advertiser* in South Carolina, was similarly despairing of the state of the workforce. 'Labour is scarce, high, and very unreliable', it said. 'None want to work for wages.' Fast-forward to 2014 and the *Germantown News* in Tennessee carried an article by a pastor that asked: 'What happened to the work ethic in America? Nobody wants to work anymore. It wasn't always like that. When I first started work as a teenager, I saw people work hard.'[2]

There is a long-standing and proud tradition of complaining about the laziness of the working population. There is, though, something in the complaint in 2022. Not because it is on the money. People do want to work, just look at the success of, for example, the gig work website Fiverr.com.[3] And, despite the claims of some, today's Zennials do want to work for the public good. US Congresswoman Haley Stevens, who was first elected to the House of

Representatives in 2018 along with 19 other Millennials – she's now 40 – told *Time* in 2020[4]: 'I think there's a little bit of a misperception that people have about Millennials: we do feel very called to service. Kids of the '90s, we grew up thinking we were going to change the world.'

But people want to work in different ways than before. This small fact has huge potential consequences. And is one of the key reasons why the upcoming transfer of wealth, power and influence needs to be navigated carefully if we are to avoid the collapse of capitalism.

The key shift I will be discussing in this book is, as mentioned above, intergenerational, so it will be practical to define some terms early on. Because there is a lot of talk about generations in modern society, but terms are often used without specificity. We hear about silent generations, golden generations, squeezed generations. Gens X, Y and Z have given way to Generation Alpha (the oldest of whom are about 12). The London 2012 Olympics aimed to 'Inspire a Generation', with mixed success.[5] The airline EasyJet has claimed an entire generation for its own. And opinion columnists the world over look to the generation gap for inspiration every single day.

So what exactly is a generation? And when we talk about generations, do we all mean the same thing?

DEFINING A GENERATION

There are several answers. A simple dictionary definition provides this: 'all of the people born and living at about the same time, regarded collectively'. In a different usage, a generation is simply the period of time, about 20 to 30 years, during which children are born and grow up, become adults, and begin to have children of their own. Meanwhile,

Herodotus – 'the father of history' if you believe Cicero or the 'father of lies' if you prefer Plutarch – used generation as a simple measure of time. 'Now three hundred generations are ten thousand years, three generations being equal to a hundred', he wrote in 430 BC.

But it is the sociological understanding of generations that generally preoccupies us in the twenty-first century. The idea that a generation is not simply a period of time or a way of arbitrarily grouping people, but that generational location points to 'certain definite modes of behaviour, feeling, and thought'. That is to say, the timing of one's birth has an impact on how we experience, and therefore understand, the world around us.

Hungarian-born sociologist Karl Mannheim's 1928 essay 'The Problem of Generations' is widely regarded[6] as the most systematic and fully developed treatment of generations from a sociological perspective. For Mannheim, generations are not fixed. They are not mere periods of time into which we all fall. They are indicators of social change and 'indispensable guides to an understanding of the structure of social and intellectual movements'.

I would tend to agree with that characterization. It seems quite clear that the timing of one's birth does matter and does have an impact on a person's political, economic and social beliefs. The simple fact that I was born in 1949 means I have a common cultural language with those born around the same time and have had different experiences and opportunities to my children, who were born in the 1980s.

There is a danger when using generational terminology that we 'flatten out the experiences of tens of millions of very different people, remove nuance from conversations, and imply commonality where there may be none'.[7] But it is also foolish to trivialize the notion of generations. The formative years of one's life do not occur in a vacuum. Exterior events have their impact, and the bigger the event, the more seismic and widespread the impact. According to one study,[8] political events between the ages of 14 and 24 have around triple the impact of events experienced later in life.[9]

With that in mind, it will be interesting, if not potentially worrying, to eventually discover the impact of Covid-19 on the generation that was coming of age during its nadir (or peak, depending on your point of view). Those schoolchildren and university students who weren't able to attend school and university for months on end. But that is for another time.

What I can, and will be, discussing here is those generations whose formative events we can at least start to examine with the benefit of some hindsight.

BOOMERS VS ZENNIALS

It is vital when looking at the origins of my own generation, Boomers, to understand quite how much of a boom there was in the post-war period. In the United States, there were 3,288,672 births in the year after the end of the Second World War, 1946 – year zero for the Boomer generation. Never before had the birth rate topped three million. It was a more than half-million increase on 1945, and a million increase on a decade earlier. By 1954, the figure was over four million, where it stayed until 1964, the last of the Boomer birth years. After that, it would not be until 1989 that US births went over four million again. But by then the total population was just shy of 247 million. In 1954, it had only just hit the 163 million mark.[10]

All of which is to say that the Boomer generation is notably large. And we had the good fortune, at least in the West, to come of age at a time of increasing affluence compared to our parents. As young adults entering the workforce for the first time, we graduated with little to no debt, and the prospect of buying a house within years was not just realistic but expected. In a recent interview with the *Financial Times*,[11] PIMCO CEO Emmanuel Roman summed the situation up pithily: 'The post-Volcker[12] years have been very good for financial markets and for our generation. I call that generational luck.'

That luck has not remained for the generations that followed. Millennials (born between 1981 and 1996) and their Zoomer comrades (for my purposes here, I am generally talking of older members of Gen Z who are now in the workforce) are, in so many ways, the sons and daughters of the 2008 financial crisis. For them, that is the original sin. That is the infection they are trying to cure.

They are digital natives, forged by the internet and unafraid to partner with it. Technology is not 'other' to these generations, but intrinsic, a fact that will give them the ability to wield the power and capital they are about to inherit in incredibly significant ways. It is because of these similarities between the generations that I have opted to discuss them collectively as Zennials. As much because I see them as allies rather than enemies, something that cannot currently be said of the relationship between Zennials and Boomers.

Zennials, to a large extent, resent Boomers, and it is quite easy to see why. From the perspective of Millennial entrepreneur Doone Roisin,[13] Boomers came of age at a hell of a time:

In a post-World War II world, the baby boomers' working and living experiences were that of great prosperity. Their parents had already made sacrifices during the war years to give them a better life and had paid all the taxes necessary to keep university tuition low, which meant as young adults entering the workforce for the first time, boomers could graduate with little to no debt. At the same time, housing was plentiful post-war, and strong labour protections meant even high-school graduates could afford to buy their first homes on a minimum hourly rate salary. These homes then continued to appreciate in value over time, and decades of economic growth followed for the boomers. So much so that by 2020, records show that the baby boomer generation held approximately 57 per cent of all wealth and assets in the U.S. economy. In comparison, Millennials held just three per cent of the country's entire wealth.

This good fortune has not, at least as far as Zennials are concerned, translated into Boomer humility. Indeed, quite the opposite. Zennial journalist, podcaster and author Olivia Petter opened a column in *The Times*[14] recently with the words: 'Another day, another opportunity to blame the world's problems on young people.' The cause of her indignation? The fact that a survey had found Zennials, or more specifically Zoomers, to be less tolerant of other people's views, leading them to be labelled 'Young Illiberal Progressives', or Yips. Petter's well-argued contention, though, was that her generation do not deserve to be simply classed as new puritans, because while they are 'more censorious than their elders, [this is] in support of people they see as vulnerable'. Their lack of tolerance is towards prejudices such as transphobia, racism, misogyny, homophobia and climate change denial, rather than groups of people. But, according to Petter, there is a crucial reason for this distinction not being clear to Boomers, who may simply look at the survey results and use them as a stick with which to beat the younger generation. The reason is that Petter's contemporaries 'have not simply grown up with social media, we've also grown up with the dialogue it creates'.[15]

So we have a situation where Boomers and Zennials cannot communicate properly – not least due to technology – and where one generation has clearly been more fortunate than another – people in their sixties in the UK are much likelier to have more than £1 million in assets than any other age group. Petter and Roisin's own generation and the generation below it have not been so fortunate as their parents in their formative years. University tuition has not been low, housing has not been plentiful and cheap, and – as far as many Zennials see it – their parents didn't so much make sacrifices as make a killing before crashing the economy.

Until 1998, full-time students in England could attend public universities completely free of charge. Now, the average annual price of most public universities in England is £9,250.[16] That means debt, and lots of it. In 2021, a Freedom of Information request uncovered that the largest amount of debt amassed by a student in England was a staggering £189,700. That was an exceptional case. But student debts around the £100,000 mark are not uncommon, and the *average* loan figure for those who graduated in 2020 was £45,060. Meanwhile, in the US, student debt has more than doubled over the last two decades.[17] Put bluntly, the debt burden on Zennial university graduates is huge compared to that of Boomers.

That debt has its impact on Zennials' prospects of ever being able to buy their own homes. With each passing year, the share of Millennial renters saying they will never own a home is increasing (it's now 22 per cent). And the percentage of 40-year-old Millennials in the US who own their own home is markedly lower than for Boomers at the same age (60 compared to 68).[18] In the UK in the past 20 years, house prices have more than trebled, causing home ownership to collapse among the young. In 1989, more than 50 per cent of those aged between 25 and 34 owned a home. By 2019, that figure had nearly halved to 28 per cent.[19]

That leaves Zennials with the prospect of renting for their entire lives, giving money to landlords – many of whom are Boomers – every month instead of paying off a mortgage that could eventually lead them to owning their own home; a major asset. In central London, where I live, the average monthly rent for a typical two-bedroom home is £1,450, and the average couple in a private tenancy in England pays 41 per cent of their income on rent, compared to 18 per cent for home owners and 30 per cent for social tenants.[20] No wonder Zennials are dissatisfied with their lot. And it's not much better when it comes to their working lives.

Zennials, certainly in the UK, are disengaging from the workplace. Or, to quote a phrase, they are 'quiet quitting'. They are 'avoiding the above and beyond, the hustle culture mentality, or what psychologists call "occupational citizenship behaviours"'.[21] They are staying in work with their heads and leaving their hearts elsewhere to other interests and passions. There is a serious need for incentivized productivity. Heartless engagement is essentially unproductive. According to Gallup's global workplace report for 2022, only 9 per cent of workers – now predominantly Zennials – in the UK were engaged or enthusiastic about their work, ranking 33rd out of 38 European countries.[22]

This is what has created the conflict between the two generations. A perceived, and real, unfairness that Boomers got lucky while Zennials have not. This has significant consequences for the future of capitalism because Zennials want things to change. They want things to be fairer. And they will certainly have no qualms about throwing out wholesale anything they think has a whiff of Boomer about it. For them, their 'ill-gotten' gains are tarnished capital.

But this tarnished capital can be polished. Boomers need to be prepared to accept that we are beneficiaries of the long bull market of quantitative easing, of a low-interest, asset-inflated world. We need to accept that there has been a disproportionate inequality in the way in which the generations have participated in this boom. Boomers will have to go the extra mile to understand the legitimate accusations of the Zennial generation and not merely dismiss these as generational whinging. Nor should Boomers stand back but they should recognize that there is a critical and essential role to play in working together to ensure, notwithstanding the apparently unfair distribution of capital in a previous generation, that capitalism retains its robust capacity to create a value but also to be mindful of the way in which prosperity is shared.

THE ORIGINAL SIN

I have been an investment banker for well over 40 years, working in the citadel of finance – the capital markets of London. I have lived through many financial crises. However, not one of them has been as profound as the shift now taking place throughout the world, precisely because it's not a purely financial shift, but a deep-rooted challenge to the philosophical underpinning of the market economy, as defined by a previous generation. It's a challenge to a long-held status quo and its effects will be greater than the post-war Bretton Woods agreements or any governmental efforts to create global financial stability.

We are facing a greater threat now to our capitalist system than even in the wake of the 2008 GFC. The current global financial system is deeply in debt, energy prices have reached unaffordable levels, and – unimaginable in a previous generation – war has broken out in Ukraine. Central banks and governments believe, as do international financial institutions, that they have the measure of these problems and can navigate the global economy through them. But it is by no means certain that this will be the case. It would further fuel intergenerational tension if, for whatever reason, the global economy is not stabilized in the next few years and growth and opportunity is impaired. In these circumstances it would again appear that the home-owning Boomer generation will be able to survive more easily than the next generation.

When I first joined the City as a banker in 1976, we were in the midst of the first sterling crisis – and it was worse than the more recent volatility for being the first. I remember being introduced on my first day to the foreign exchange trading floor and watching sterling tumble on an old-fashioned monitor. Unimaginably and humiliatingly the Chancellor of the Exchequer had to go cap-in-hand to the IMF for financial help to prevent a decline in sterling. Fear was palpable as losses piled up. I can smell it even now. The senior trader looked at my CV and saw that I had read theology at Cambridge. When I asked him what could be done to arrest the decline in the pound, I expected an economic answer. Instead, with an exhausted and fearful look he said, 'Pray! ... You might have more influence than the economists and traders!' In this, I recognized a fundamental truth that economic intelligence alone is a limiting factor in a crisis. Underlying political and social forces, if not theology, drive the financial system. The capital markets do not exist in isolation from the rest of human behaviour and society; they share its pathology. All crises are the same in fear-inducing volatility; each crisis is radically different in how we navigate it.

Since then, I have worked in numerous capacities, chairing various international institutions during some of the major financial crises of our time: the great crash of 1987, the dot-com bubble of 2000, and of course the GFC. As previously mentioned, the GFC is distinct as one of the formative events of the Zennials' lifetimes (certainly in the US; the other would be 9/11); a lightning-rod moment. It impacted on them in a life-changing way and sowed seeds of doubt in the trustworthiness of major institutions, especially the banking system. They were dealt a bad hand that they have neither forgotten nor forgiven. In a spectacular way, capital markets had slipped their ethical moorings of serving the common good; finance had become fractured. The reaction of this generation, scarred by the breakdown of trust and the effects of the GFC on their families, fuelled a critical, and at times iconoclastic, response to the global market economy.

A couple of months into the GFC, the Occupy anti-capitalist movement was camped outside St Paul's Cathedral, with hundreds aggressively protesting against the London Stock Exchange. Fear was in the air – of vandalism or violent attacks on bankers and the stock exchange. This fear led to calls to forcibly remove the entire protest. In the midst of it, I had the privilege of being asked by the then Bishop of London to intervene and try to find common ground between the City's financial fathers and those demonstrating. And as I went into the camps, I was profoundly struck by the intensity of the outrage. One question was fired at me immediately: 'If capitalism is so good for you, why isn't it good for me? Why must my generation suffer because greedy bankers have fucked up the world?' Around me were placards that read: 'If capitalism is so good, why can't my generation find homes and jobs?' This question has haunted me ever since and continues to impress upon me the urgency with which my generation needs to respond.

Many have asked, 'Will this just peter out?' I don't think so. It's been over a decade since Occupy and things have intensified. These are not just feckless youth or flower-power drop-outs – certainly not any more – but a global collective of highly sophisticated and impassioned individuals, empowered by new technology to reach a wide audience, willing to take to the streets, press and social media to bring about the change they believe in. Moreover, I think they are harbingers of a legitimate generational vision, which is beginning to be realized in the marketplace as the colossal generational capital handover takes place.

Their vision won't just be small tweaks to banking regulations; it will be radical, pervasive and wholesale. The GFC was seen as a failure of the entire financial ecosystem and the Zennials began a process of questioning the nature of capitalism itself. This kickstarted a trend, not from outside the marketplace, but embedded within it. These Zennials will be inheriting the major financial institutions of the world and have begun to reject the idea that there is a set 'way that things work'. 'That's just how it is, get on with it' is not acceptable to this generation, because they have seen what happens when that kind of attitude is allowed to prosper. They want to shape the future of capitalism on their own terms. They want to work in different ways that encapsulate different principles from their parents, and they will have the financial means to make this a reality. And with their spinnakers of outrage billowing it would be wrong for Boomers simply to become passive observers. A sea change is needed and it requires all hands to navigate these uncharted waters well.

WILL ZENNIALS NOT CHANGE?

There is an assumption among many in my generation that the iconoclasm displayed by many Zennials towards the institutions we built will disappear as they get older. And, more specifically, when they become beneficiaries of the Great Wealth Transfer. This is the attitude behind the famous maxim, often misattributed to Winston Churchill, that 'if you're not a liberal at 20, you have no heart; if you're not a conservative at 40, you have no brain'. As a recent piece in the *Daily Telegraph* (incidentally written by the journalist Michael Deacon, a member of Generation X, the cohort that sits between Boomers and Millennials) predicted, while now it may be open season on Boomers – who get blamed for everything from wealth inequality to the shortage of affordable housing – once they inherit wealth, today's left-wing Millennials may suddenly decide they aren't so keen on socialism after all.

I would be extremely wary of making that assumption. For one thing, Boomers making a sweeping claim that Zennials will 'grow out' of their left-wing ideals is exactly the kind of patronizing attitude that has served to drive a wedge between the two groups. For another, the assumption misunderstands the fact that the Zennial is a fundamentally different being from the Boomer, with a different outlook on the way the world should work. And their anti-capitalist (or, less dramatically, capitalist-sceptic) tendencies are not necessarily going to simply disappear with age or inherited wealth. This is not a criticism or a compliment but a necessary thing to understand. Because Zennial idealism will have a huge impact on the future of capitalism. It is something that will need to be directed, even curbed at times; but it is not something that can be forced out of them.

As James Marriott pointed out in a *Times* piece in early 2023, Zennials in English-speaking countries specifically are unlikely to do a political volte-face as they grow older. He wrote[23]:

If you are young, idealistic and anxious to know whether the purity of your left-wing principles will survive the disappointments of middle age, you might pay attention to the language being spoken around you. If you can hear English there is a better chance that your youthful socialism will remain uncorrupted. In Britain, America, Australia, New Zealand and Canada, millennials are defying ancient political laws and failing to become more right-wing as they age. Modern 35-year-olds in Britain and America are, according to a recent analysis in the *Financial Times*, 'by far the least conservative 35-year-olds in recorded history'.

The same is not true in mainland Europe. It seems that in France, Italy, Germany and Spain, 'young people still follow ancient routes of political migration, voting for more right-wing parties as they get older'.[24]

So the Boomer generation, particularly in the English-speaking world, will need to find new ways of engaging with the upcoming generation. The days of the command-and-control management structure have died but the new form of engagement is not yet fully defined. But it will have as its central driving force the need for a more sensitive approach based on collaboration and a greater openness to consultation and inclusion in the way in which decisions are made. The most enlightened are already pursuing this and recognize the need to understand at a very deep level, but also to be confident in challenging the underlying idealistic passions of the generation.

Bear in mind that, despite the term Millennial still consistently being used to refer to young people in our society, the oldest in that generation are now in their forties and the youngest their mid-twenties. Many Zennials are 'grown up' and they are not necessarily becoming more conservative. Indeed, a recent report from the Institute of Economic Affairs (a market economy think-tank) suggests they're not going to become so any time soon. The report's author, Dr Kristian Niemietz, says that 'over the past five years or so, there have been a flurry of surveys showing a rising popularity of socialist ideas among Millennials (as well as, increasingly, Generation Z). A generation, if not two generations, has turned against capitalism.'

This is the concern that is at the heart of this book. Because we are at a pivotal point in the emergence of a new way in which capital is earned, invested and deployed. The question before us is whether the Zennials' values will be forcibly imposed on the world, or whether we can work together to move forward. Because make no mistake, Zennials want change. The stark truth underlying this generational restlessness is the fact that, unlike previous generations, each one of whom could expect to inherit a better standard of living than the previous one, this generation will almost certainly not.

A good illustration of this fact comes from looking at a super-rich Zennial. They are few and far between, certainly when compared with the number of super-rich Boomers, but they do exist. Thirty-year-old Marlene Engelhorn is one of them. A recent *New York Times* profile of her was headlined: 'She's Inheriting Millions of Euros. She Wants Her Wealth Taxed Away.'

Ms Engelhorn is a partial heir to her family's multibillion-dollar fortune, which originated with Friedrich Engelhorn, who in 1865 founded BASF, one of the world's largest chemical companies. She was raised in Vienna, lacking, she says, any awareness of class privilege.[25] Now, though, she is 'part of a growing movement of young, leftist millionaires who say they want governments to take a much larger share of their inherited wealth, arguing that these unearned fortunes should be democratically allocated by the state'.[26]

She is a co-founder of a group called Tax Me Now and has committed to giving away at least 90 per cent of her inheritance. But she is adamant she wants it taken from her in the form of tax rather than as a philanthropic donation. This attitude to taxation specifically is a fascinating insight into the difference between Zennials and Boomers because it is effectively about removing choice. Most Boomers would baulk at the idea of the state taking away more of their wealth than absolutely necessary. But Marlene Engelhorn, while far from the typical Zennial, is reflective of a generation more willing to put their trust in the centralization of resources, perhaps foolishly.

'I am the product of an unequal society,' she says. And she is not alone, with groups of pro-tax millionaires expanding rapidly recently 'driven by what Ms. Engelhorn calls "next gens of wealth" who have a different approach than many of their parents'.[27]

This different Zennial approach is the shift I am talking about and is what is going to transform capitalism. The example of Ms Engelhorn perfectly illustrates the eagerness of her generation to completely throw out the rulebook and make transformational changes, possibly to their own detriment. She is not merely looking to ensure that her generation's millionaires do the right thing philanthropically. Indeed, this is the opposite of what she wants. She wants the system transformed.

This type of transformation will happen worldwide in the Zennial age, and if we are not prepared to deal with it, things will break.

I, personally, reject the assumptions underlying Engelhorn's anger. This is precisely the area in which Boomers should not lose their confidence in being vigorous in debate and robust in analysis to point to the dangers underlying this view, which views taxation rather than innovation and value creation as being the central requirement for the new emerging capitalist system.

2

THE CRISIS IN CAPITALISM

In November 1790, the Irish statesman Edmund Burke published a political pamphlet entitled *Reflections on the Revolution in France*. In it he assessed a century of revolution, bloodshed and social reorganization. The French Revolution had upended European society, America had also won their independence from the British sovereign, and the world order had been rewritten. There were great hopes and dreams for a Republican future and many were asking fundamental questions about how we ought to live in a state. How ought citizens relate to one another? How should a country recover from the instability of revolution? What are the main dynamics at play that makes society go around?

Burke was writing in the century when one of the most influential political theories was Jean-Jacques Rousseau's social contract: the idea that societies function through mutual consent between the individuals of a state, and between the population and the governing sovereign (monarch or otherwise). Basically, we trust each other because it is mutually beneficial, and we trust governing bodies with the expectation that they will secure the freedoms that are our due. Burke, however, perceived another layer through this. He wrote that, in fact, 'the state ... is ... a partnership not only between those who are living, but between those who are living, those who are dead, and those who are to be born'. The true social contract did not lie between sovereign and people, but between generations. Society can only hold together if there is generational trust.

What a phrase for our time: generational trust. Because, as I have said, it would be an understatement to suggest there has been a breakdown of that trust and mutual respect between Boomers and Zennials. Indeed, generational tensions are at a breaking point. It is heartbreaking, cynical, and a threat to the future of capitalism and, in turn, our world.

THE BREAKING OF THE FOUNDATIONS

The formative years of my life, as I grew up, were shaped by the zeitgeist of the 1960s. The decade that tore up the limitations, borders and perimeters of the old world. Nothing was off-limits. It was a me-first world that proudly proclaimed that all the boundaries had gone. And all this coincided with the exceptional post-war economic boom in the West. In the 1980s, 1990s and 2000s the dominant trend was rising prosperity. At its worst, this became the loads-a-money caricature. It is no wonder the 1980s was called the Decade of Excess. Financial markets were deregulated to create greater competition and monetary policy was eased to levels that led to the current indigestion and danger in the capital markets.

But we all know how that story ended.

I can remember the moment exactly. I was in my office when the rumours first started. There had been whispers for months, but there were always whispers. This time, however, it felt terrifyingly real. The year was 2008. The Global Financial Crisis, the most serious financial crisis since 1929's Wall Street Crash, was upon us. A result of the bursting of the US housing bubble, it was a crisis that saw US GDP decline by 4.3 per cent and unemployment increase from 5 to 10 per cent, and its impact was global.

From my office window I could see the City of London as usual – the hushed, almost churchy quiet and the rows of gleaming buildings. It looked horribly like the calm before the storm, as if everything was on the verge of breaking. Within days, Lehman Brothers would collapse. The image of bankers with their cardboard boxes would fill screens around the world. In turn, that would trigger the meltdown of the financial system on both sides of the Atlantic, undercutting the very foundations of our modern economy. Banks running out of money, employees unable to be paid, families being evicted from their homes. The mechanics of society screeching to a deathly halt. As I saw it all ahead of us that day, I felt a growing sickness.

I was international chairman of one of the most prestigious investment banks in the world. When it came to the financial universe, at least, I had reached as far as it was possible to go. But that day was like nothing I'd ever experienced before. There is a tendency in life to imagine that the status quo is permanent, almost a fact of nature. But, as I stared around the magnificent buildings, I knew that the opposite was true. We had made all of this. The banks, the financial system, even the notion of paper money in the first place – all of it was merely a human invention. We had invented the means of our own destruction. Soon there would be panic spreading through global capital markets. Soon the hours, days and weeks spent bunkered down in the office with phones ringing from every corner, desperately trying to find a way through. All that and more was still to come.

But in that moment – that singular minute of time – there was just a fragile calm. The sense of a world held in suspense, waiting for the axe to fall. The knowledge that centuries of human progress had brought us to this point. Scientifically, we knew more about the world than any generation before us. Technologically, we had created elaborate systems that spanned the globe. Our planet was connected like never before, a dream unthinkable even one or two generations ago. And now that very connectivity was about to undo us, sending panic ricocheting to all corners of the earth before anyone could stop it. The system was about to show itself for what it was. Something impermanent. Illusory. Nothing more than elaborate smoke and mirrors.

The foundation of our modern society, the rock on which our system was built, trickled away like sand. As the 2000s faded into memory and we entered into the swing of the 2010s, I began to be profoundly struck by how the events of 2008 had impacted on the generation who were just coming of age at the time – the 'Millennials'. There is no doubt that this generation, and the one to follow, Gen Z, were profoundly impacted by the Global Financial Crisis. There is no end of articles written about this phenomenon. There is a sense that they have been dealt a bad hand in life, that the sins of their fathers have been borne by them. They saw the lives of parents or of their older siblings ripped apart by the financial collapse, fuelled by mismanagement, group-think and greed. The Zennial generation became one that is more aware of injustices and failings of the past. One that's more outspoken against people in positions of power. But it didn't end there.

ADDING INSULT TO INJURY

Twelve years later, I found myself again face to face with the collapse of the status quo. Any semblance of regeneration and rebuilding that had taken place had once again slipped from under our feet. Of course I am talking about the Covid-19 pandemic. Once again our ongoing connectedness and global integration had been the catalyst to our undoing – this time, epidemiological rather than financial. The Zennial generation have experienced two 'once-in-a-lifetime' events in less than two decades. That, by any measure, really is a bad 'bad hand'.

The year 2020 was not a good one for juniors in any corporate firm. Older Millennials will have been shielded from the decimation of the job market, but if you found yourself as a mid-to-late-twenties professional, you would have felt the brakes put on your career and the wheels start to screech. Pay was cut, promotions were held up, and networking opportunities were lost – and that's if you were lucky. If you weren't, you would have been furloughed or would have been cut altogether. If you found yourself as an early-twenties Gen Z graduate, you will have experienced one of the worst job markets in a generation. The budding possibilities of early career will have been trampled on. Meanwhile, the asset-rich Boomer generation has massively benefited from inflation and the stock markets rallying in unprecedented ways in the last 20 years, despite the 2008 crash.

As such, is it any real surprise that Zennials have lost faith in the capitalist system? And lost faith to the point that they are deciding to drop out of the game altogether. 'People are losing their faith in the future,'[1] believes Joel Kotkin, Presidential Fellow in Urban Futures at Chapman University. So much so that they are not even taking part in the processes that could improve things. In the world's democracies, voter turnout has dropped from an average 80 per cent in the 1980s to closer to 60 per cent today, largely due to younger generations' refusal, perhaps understandably, to take part. Kotkin's prognosis is worrying, but crystallizes perfectly the need for a route back to engagement for Zennials.

'Capitalism certainly is not in good stead. A strong majority of people in 28 countries around the world believe capitalism does more harm than good', he writes. 'In the future, the disaffected masses could find themselves living more like prisoners than citizens. Avoiding that outcome requires finding ways to replace disaffection with ambition and a commitment to human progress.'

If Zennials are to engage with capitalism in the same way as their parents, capitalism needs to change. Zennials need to be given not just a reason to participate in society but a reason to want to. A generation without capital can never be capitalists. Nor can a generation of renters looking enviously at their parents' generation of homeowners and asset accumulators from which they have been excluded. But a generation that believes there is greater benefit in working together to repair capitalism than there is in staying in their silos railing against it can be galvanized to use the capital they will inherit in new and exciting ways.

WHY THE ANTI-CAPITALISM?

Zennials have had it tough, and still have it tough. I cannot deny that the capitalism that I experienced, and to some degree championed, through my working life has accentuated intergenerational inequality and imbalance. And since 2008 and now 2020, the balance sheet of humanity is not going to be paid by my generation, it will be paid by theirs. Young people are calling out: 'If it is so good, why isn't it delivering for us and the people we care about?!' To this charge, simply referring to the cold, analytic utilitarian claims that 'capitalism has brought more untold prosperity to billions of people than any system in the past' simply will not do. It won't help when whatever moral credibility big business and financial institutions had is dead in the water.

And yet, there are many of my generation who believe that young people today are entitled, ungrateful, impatient good-for-nothings who complain about everything. Or as Frank Furedi puts it in his book *Why Borders Matter*, Millennials are 'too infantilised, too floppy, too incapable of independent thought to be much use to anyone'. Whether it is in the workplace, or in rearing families, or simply the act of 'getting on with it', the Zennial generation are seen as incapable of doing anything worthwhile. The Boomer looks down on them. After all, life wasn't a walk in the park for them. They had to face the grind and the churn. Success only comes to those willing to start at the bottom and deal with the rubbish jobs. Zennials simply think the world will be handed to them on a silver platter.

This is incredibly unfair and simply will not do. I have coached and mentored Zennials throughout this time of massive change in social norms, technological change and economic dislocation, and I have learned much from them. I have found them to be, at heart, a deeply prophetic generation, willing to scrutinize every angle of the prism of society and call out a future that is not yet realized. The watchmen of humanity are facing an identity crisis. The young generation is making a significant contribution towards the reassessment of what our common life should look like in a world in which globalization has been actualized, pressing ahead in social action and environmental concern even at the cost of their own potential prosperity. It is admirable.

However, this state of affairs has not helped the emotional health of the Zennial either. For them, there is a sense that Boomers have been poor stewards of the world, economy and society, and that every single injustice and evil that assails us today is a result of selfishness and money-hungry corporate ambitions. Legitimate or not, this has engendered a deep sense of bitterness, resentment and sometimes even hatred towards the older generation. This also will not do.

In the 2020 revised edition of *Speeches that Changed the World*, the editors included Greta Thunberg's now famous speech at the UN Climate Action Summit in the summer of 2019. In it, she gave a withering address that made headlines around the world as she accused world leaders of gross negligence and complacency in the face of the urgent climate crisis.

The speech starts:

> This is all wrong. I shouldn't be up here. I should be back in school on the other side of the ocean. Yet you all come to us young people for hope. How dare you! You have stolen my dreams and my childhood with your empty words. And yet I'm one of the lucky ones. People are suffering. People are dying. Entire ecosystems are collapsing. We are in the beginning of a mass extinction, and all you can talk about is money and fairy tales of eternal economic growth. How dare you!

And it finishes:

> You are failing us. But the young people are starting to understand your betrayal. The eyes of all future generations are upon you. And if you choose to fail us, I say: we will never forgive you. We will not let you get away with this. Right here, right now is where we draw the line. The world is waking up. And change is coming, whether you like it, or not.

This language is unquestionably moving. It is motivating and compelling. It is powerful and has the potential to shift the needle of human society. But it is also angry, full of rage, and spiteful; full of great expectations as well as great condemnation. These are the words that made headlines across the globe and inspired a generation to take to the streets; words that have raised questions in corporate boardrooms across the world; words that capture the zeitgeist of a generation – a deep heart-cry that culminates in the passionate assertion: 'We will never forgive you.'

We have broken each other's truth. Pope Francis's 2020 Encyclical *Fratelli tutti* reminds us that 'the earth is lent to each generation, to be handed on to the generation to follow'. Today, the older generations are scared to hand on the earth to those they feel are not worthy of it, while the emerging generation feel they are being handed a ruined creation. Edmund Burke's 'Partnership of Generations' feels a million miles away.

So how do we fix that? How do we create a world in which Boomers don't patronize Zennials, and Zennials don't spit spite at Boomers, forever blaming them for their lot in life? How do we create a genuine partnership of generations? Because we absolutely must. We must all be on the same page if the upcoming once-in-a-generation transfer – of power, of capital, of influence – is to be carried out smoothly and effectively and, crucially, with capitalism still intact.

AVOIDING THE WHIPLASH OF PROGRESS

The old world is gone. The way things used to work is not coming back. The attitudes that used to prevail will not be respawned. That's progress. And it's a good thing. But it can also be jarring, especially when progress happens as quickly as it has in the last century. (The pandemic has additionally reshaped global perspectives at every level: financial, social and institutional.)

In his wildly successful book *Sapiens: A Brief History of Humankind*, Yuval Noah Harari imagines a Spanish peasant falling asleep in AD 1000 and waking up 500 years later, 'to the din of Columbus' sailors boarding the *Niña*, *Pinta* and *Santa María*'.[2] The world into which our unnamed hero awoke, speculates Harari, would have seemed to him 'quite familiar'.

'But had one of Columbus' sailors fallen into a similar slumber and woken up to the ringtone of a twenty-first-century iPhone, he would have found himself in a world strange beyond comprehension. "Is this heaven?" he might well have asked himself. "Or perhaps – hell?"'

I believe that within this idea lies the unique friction between Boomers and Zennials today. And the unique threat posed to the status quo as a result. Because never before have two cohorts that are, in relative historical terms, of the same era, been so distinctly separated by their generational environments. Centuries of progress have occurred in mere decades. Harari imagined someone who fell asleep and woke up 500 years later. But what about someone who fell asleep in 1960, 1970, or even 1980, and woke up today? To a world in which an iPhone has 100,000 times the processing power of the computer that first landed man on the moon.[3] To a world in which you don't need to leave your house for anything. To a world of the internet, and social media – a term only coined in 1994. This is the world of now, one that the Boomer oversaw the creation of, but unlike the Zennial, is not a native in.

And so I say to Zennials, be understanding of that.

'The past is a foreign country; they do things differently there', wrote L. P. Hartley at the opening of his classic 1953 novel *The Go-Between*. This is perhaps an instructive way to try to sympathize with the Boomer from a Zennial perspective. By trying to imagine what it might be like in 50 years' time when looking back to now.

Zennials, believe me when I say that this is a wholly different world to the one my contemporaries and I knew when we were your age. It's not that some things are different; everything is different. The way we live, the way we work, the way we interact. We have benefited hugely from the changes that have taken place. But that does not make the whiplash of rapid progress any less awkward, especially when we know that the control we had over it is starting to lessen. To which you might be inclined to say: 'Thank goodness. You've had control for long enough, it's our turn now, to fix what you've broken.'

But, perhaps strangely, now is the time to be humble. You are about to inherit the earth and you have big ideas for it. But be aware that it is difficult to give something up, especially something of such significance. That is what my generation is about to do; and we will have no control over what happens to it. We also fear, because of the antipathy between our two generations, that our hard-earned knowledge – our hindsight – may be wasted because you do not trust that it is worth anything. Please know that it is. That for the benefit of you as well as us, it is valuable that we work together well, and benefit from each other.

And to the Boomer: be aware. The influence and voice of Zennials will not decrease. This is not simply a youthful rebellious trend that will peter out in a couple of years. There is an increasing realization of the inequitable distribution between generations. For Zennials, it has become prohibitively difficult to buy a house, one of the hallmarks of wealth generation for private individuals. Not only that, but as we, the Boomers, grow older and live longer, it will cost the Zennials to pay off society's debts. Above this, we have to realize that our generation has been the beneficiary of cheap electricity, and fast-growth strategies. These avenues are no longer open to the emerging generation, whose hands are tied by both their conscience and ecological necessity to seek out newer (and more expensive) means of generating the energy required to build a world for themselves. In fact, one estimate puts the cost of decarbonizing the world at $100 trillion.[4] This burden and discontent will express itself not only through outbursts of condemnation and hatred, as above, but also through destabilizing actions in our world.

THE CRISIS OF CAPITALISM IN ACTION

I can't help being reminded of the GameStop Stock incident in early 2021. It took my world by storm. This was when a frenzied outbreak of stock trading occurred throughout the world in which 'small investors', many of whom were Zennials, clubbed together to use new digital trading platforms to reverse short positions accumulated by hedge funds in companies such as GameStop.

Short positions are taken by hedge funds that sell shares in the expectation that they will go down, essentially making money by betting on companies to fail. The collective action was organized on a Reddit forum called WallStreetBets, and an army of these small investors with various motives decided to purchase shares in significant amounts, thereby driving the share price up and causing the short position to be closed, with enormous losses suffered by the hedge funds. In fact, within a month, GameStop shares were up 1,500 per cent.

What makes this striking is that the small individual investors were not financial investors. Few had formal training but they had enough information at their fingertips, and the connectivity, to be able to pull off very sophisticated stock-trading tactics. This was an almighty F.U. to the system that they believed had dealt them a bad hand at the expense of a previous generation. When regulators tried to stop these activities, the small investors, disillusioned with a system that they believed was supportive of Wall Street institutions, turned against them. Much of this is reminiscent of the 2000s and the dot-com bubble. The difference is that the players are just ordinary people. With the advent of platforms that have democratized the financial institutions to the ordinary person, more people are enabled to become full participants in the financial system and, regardless of risk, start reacting against the inequality that has become obvious to them. GameStop was a brick-and-mortar video game retailer. It was struggling as the industry was moving online.

It would be naïve not to recognize the motivations of the ringleaders of the movement. This was about perceived injustice and sticking it to the man. Zennials felt excluded from a financial system that had enriched a previous generation at their expense. And so, with their newfound tools and collective organization, they could go to war against the old guard. If this war continues, it will be good for nobody.

Michael Fraley, one of the Reddit ringleaders, said in an interview that 'if we could all be making money while also undoing a very rich person's wealth, it's even more empowering'. Melvin Capital, one of the hedge funds caught in this wildfire, was forced to take extremely painful losses totalling $6.8 billion that threatened its very future.[5] Bill Gross, the founder of PIMCO, one of the largest debt funds, likened the activities to a 'populist political uprising'. It was the sheer magnitude of the collective activity that so unsettled both regulators and investors and, naturally, the hedge funds.

Investment clubs have been around for generations. The difference is that this crisis was sparked by a highly sophisticated group of Zennial investors able to corral a large number of unsophisticated ones in the retail space to join in the frenzy, to make a political statement and make money. Anti-Wall Street movements and sentiments have always been around, but this made us wake up.

THE CRYPTO FACTOR

Cryptocurrency is also capitalizing on this extraordinary sentiment and generational discontent. Cryptocurrency is more than just a digital alternative to gold or a wealth-storing asset. Sure, Bitcoin and blockchain technology does allow massive international transactions to be made safely and securely, at a distance – this clearly has a competitive advantage over something like gold, which is heavy, difficult to transport, and fairly easy to steal. It is also already the case that most of our wealth and finances is now represented as digital calculations.

You don't think about your wealth in terms of canvas bags of gold coins with a big dollar sign on them. No, your wealth is represented by the balance you see on your online banking screen or the spreadsheet that tracks your assets. It may very well be the case that crypto is the future that formalizes and eradicates the distinction between what is physical and what is digital.

However, the allure of cryptocurrency today lies not in its efficacy. Instead, cryptocurrency is a protest movement. It is a movement of a generation saying that 'the way you used to do things', the *ancien régime* if you will, is crumbling and that a new story is establishing itself. It is the democratization of finance. This process has not been without its difficulties, particularly recently when there has been a collapse across the board of crypto as the tech meltdown has gathered speed.

As I write this, crypto is in crisis after the implosion of FTX, one of the world's largest cryptocurrency exchange platforms. At its peak, FTX was valued at $32 billion. But on 11 November 2022, the company filed for bankruptcy; its demise, according to one commentator, combining 'The insanity of Theranos, speed of Lehman and scale of Enron.'[6] The entire crypto space is in free-fall. Bitcoin, the world's biggest cryptocurrency, plummeted about 65 per cent during 2022. And from a record high of $3 trillion in November 2021, the entire cryptocurrency market is now valued at below $1 trillion.[7]

At the heart of the crash was FTX's 30-year-old founder and former CEO Sam Bankman-Fried – also known as SBF – whose net worth dropped by billions virtually overnight. Just a few weeks before the crisis, at the Future Investment Initiative conference in Riyadh – colloquially referred to as 'Davos in the Desert' – I spent some time with SBF. I recognized him to be worth tens of billions of dollars; a crypto magnate, or king, even. I was captivated by him. He was engaging, with a slightly strange voice, curly unkempt hair, and wearing a t-shirt at a very formal, small and exclusive dinner. A number of people were dancing around him, no doubt wanting to invest with him.

A month after that dinner, where I was mesmerized by this 30-year-old Zennial and his achievements, everything melted away for Bankman-Fried. After FTX filed for bankruptcy, he was extradited to the United States facing criminal charges. In his testimony to the US House of Representatives Committee on Financial Services his opening comment was very simple: 'I would like to start by formally stating, under oath: I fucked up.'[8]

Unusual. By any standards. But probably not to a Zennial steeped in the culture of oversharing. However, the person appointed by the court to oversee the bankruptcy, John Ray, made a significant comment[9]: 'This isn't sophisticated whatsoever. This is just plain old embezzlement. Old school.'

In these two interchanges the Boomer/Zennial narrative became clear to me. The FTX saga is not the first of its kind. There's been Bernie Madoff, Wirecard, Enron. But all of them were in the Boomer generation. This is the takedown of a very high-profile Zennial, and he was taken down for the principal reason that there was no monitoring by a senior person of his enthusiasm, direction or motivation.

In simple terms, there was very little control of any kind. FTX staff were recording transactions on Slack, an office instant-messaging app. The accounts were on software used by small businesses and independent operators. There was no oversight from an experienced board of directors. Ray complained that there was 'literally no record-keeping whatsoever'. Whatever the rights and wrongs of the situation are, they will be determined by a court. But it is clear to me that, had use been made of the hindsight, experience and knowledge of a group of older people, who would have put in place the due processes, clear corporate procedures and risk controls that come naturally to my generation of corporate executives, this disaster could have been avoided. It was not. And those who have experience of how rapidly marketplaces can destroy new ideas and new fads when reality hits will know how important this is.

It is worth noting a couple more specific comments that SBF made in his statement to the House Financial Services Committee: 'I bit off more than I could chew. And ended up failing to focus on risk management.' He blamed a busy schedule that made him 'less grounded in operational details'. These failures would have been perfectly well catered for if there had been a respect for an older generation and for those who might have been able to help him at an earlier stage to avoid these pitfalls. The consequences are dangerous, as millions of dollars of value have been destroyed and many people will be facing severe financial consequences as a result. But the lesson is clear to me: that, particularly in new and innovative industries, the capitalist system works well when there is close cooperation with an experienced generation that has seen tech bubbles and other crashes and is able to help and encourage, but also to coach, comment, control and put systems in place to avoid this very sort of thing happening.

It is a cautionary tale *par excellence*. Bankman-Fried has, understandably, not been characterized well in the wake of the crisis. In an amusing but not wholly inaccurate explainer of the situation aimed at five-year-olds in *New York* magazine, Lane Brown wrote[10]: 'A silly-haired wizard sold magic beans. The villagers loved it! Until they stopped believing in magic and demanded their money back, only to find out that the wizard had already spent it.'

In one respect, SBF was a typical Zennial. He wanted to do well and to do good. He was a massive donor to the Democratic Party and to a wide range of charities which resonated with the Zennial mindset. A flawed character, yes. And a flawed financial model.

Zennials predominate and are the evangelists of crypto (94 per cent of all cryptocurrency buyers are Gen Z or Millennials[11]). And so it is unsurprising that responsibility for its demise is being placed into their hands. It was just a bunch of young jocks in the Bahamas punting around and not knowing what they were doing. Possibly fair enough. Indeed, Zennials would do well to heed the rise and fall of SBF. As I have said, a few cooler heads with some experience and the benefit of years of hindsight could have helped in averting the crisis that befell FTX. Here we have the perfect example of where Zennials and Boomers working together could have been beneficial for all.

But it is necessary to say that this is not the end for crypto, despite what some might be saying. 'The fall of FTX could be the moment that really kicks off the broader decline – maybe even demise – of cryptocurrency,' Bankrate's James Royal told CNBC at the time of the crisis.[12] But I do not see it like that. Goldman Sachs is trying to enter the game following the crisis, seeing an opportunity to pick up business and make long-term gains.[13] As I observed earlier, crypto is a Zennial protest movement, and while it may be alien to Boomers, potentially hugely risky, and perhaps still tanking as you read this, it is not going away.

'Since their inception Bitcoin, Ethereum, and their epigoni have been dismissed as a scam, a ponzi, a bubble, a fad, tulips', the novelist Tibor Fischer recently wrote in *The Spectator*.[14] 'But however you regard them – as an asset, a commodity, a currency, a store of value, a bank, a security or a hybrid of these things – they're now here to stay. Ask a banker.' I am a banker, and I agree.

Understanding crypto as best as possible, rather than dismissing it, is vital to understanding the future of capitalism. And understanding its attraction to Zennials as a tool for democratizing finance, for removing gatekeepers, is vital too.

Crypto, decentralized finance, non-fungible tokens (NFTs) – these are quintessentially Zennial phenomena. Forged in response to the status quo, they are instinctively mistrusted by Boomers, specifically because they have been built and developed by the 'first of the laptop nomads'.[15] But the laptop nomads aren't going anywhere. They are multiplying. And every Zennial who decides crypto is the thing for them is another person rejecting traditional financial products.

THE NEW GOLD STANDARD

Plenty of the wealth that is about to be passed from my generation to Zennials will be piled into cryptocurrencies;

and the crypto evangelists will be those in power. That is just the state of things. It is not a suggestion of what will happen; it is what will happen. And while the current crisis that has overwhelmed the crypto system is enormous and destructive, it will not kill off what many Boomers regard as a scam. I believe it's here to stay and, like any commodity, it's trying to find a stable equilibrium. So it is best to understand the phenomenon and try to engage with it. From both sides.

Zennials also need to understand the caution with which their elders approach something that is so alien. They have good reason to be suspicious of it. And Zennials would do well to perhaps take on some of that caution themselves and not blindly follow where the crypto bros lead. Because it has already become clear that the process of democratizing finance will be a turbulent one.

This is a story where it isn't gold that rules, but it is these blockchain structures that hold value – where crypto rules. It is a generation saying, 'You may think that digital currencies are completely worthless, but they are just as innately worthless as gold is. We will not let your definition of what is "valuable" continue to keep us down. We will create our own value in our new world.' It's also the story of technology fighting against the previous, more rigid generation that will reluctantly be dragged into the new world of cryptocurrency. In fact, I've got my hands on a little bit of Bitcoin and Ethereum to hedge my bets, and I know other Boomers who are now tiptoeing into cryptocurrencies, albeit with some hesitation.

This contest between the old and the new story is still being waged, particularly in the high volatility of the crypto space as we speak. Warren Buffet and Charlie Munger, the Chairman and Vice Chairman of Berkshire Hathaway, have come out swinging against cryptocurrency in recent years. If there was ever a person that represented 'the establishment' of the financial institutions, it would be Warren Buffet, one of the most successful and reputable investors of our generation. In 2018, he called the whole project 'a delusion, basically', and said he saw 'no unique value' in Bitcoin, which, he suggested, was 'attracting charlatans'. This came after Bitcoin's value tumbled 80 per cent from trading at $20,000 dollars down to approximately $3,500 in a matter of days. It was a moment of victory for the old establishment.

However, that was in 2018, and it wasn't the end of the story. In 2020 and 2021 there was a frantic and astronomical increase in value across the entire cryptocurrency space as ordinary people, particularly young people, began to dip their toes into investing. The same forces that drove up GameStop shares also drove the crypto market to the point that all-time highs were being set for Bitcoin and other cryptocurrencies like Ethereum on a weekly basis.

This didn't faze the leaders at Berkshire Hathaway in their disdain for the whole project, but their tune had slightly changed. At the May 2021 annual meeting, Charlie Munger launched into a scathing moral indictment of cryptocurrency, calling 'the whole damn development disgusting and contrary to the interests of civilisations'. He said he didn't welcome 'a currency so useful to kidnappers and extortionists' and suggested that the entire thing was 'created out of thin air'. Zennials smile at what appears to them naiveties. After all, the number of US dollars that are transported in suitcases in the black market are probably as extensive as any misuse of crypto. At least in the case of crypto every transaction is recorded.

The response to crypto from the old world had gone from 'this is a complete joke' to 'this is a dangerous development and must not be allowed to continue'. Bitcoin as it stands, and crypto in general, is clearly too volatile. It is still difficult to monetize and it suffers from instability, as became abundantly clear during 2022. But these are the early stages of new collective forms of activity being developed. The generational clash is 'real' and 'serious' rather than an aberration. The Boomer's voice needs to be heard, both recognizing the new reality of cryptocurrency and blockchain, and vigorously advocating for regulation to protect consumers and investors in the face of what will be strong resistance from the crypto natives.

For the younger generations, cryptocurrency and short squeeze stocks such as GameStop and AMC are a gateway to get out of their dire straits and an opportunity to reduce the generational inequality they feel. It is a way they can force money to change hands between generations. This is the appeal, and this is what is being fought out in the stock markets and the cryptocurrency exchanges. After all, Charlie Munger isn't wrong when he said that the whole thing is 'created out of thin air'. But the truth is, to a large extent, all money and value is 'created out of thin air' through the creation of credit by the banking system.

At some point in the past, we collectively decided that gold and other precious metals and stones would be a good way to determine wealth and store it. And then, instead of carrying around heavy backpacks of gold, we decided to create banks to centralize it and give out bonds and promissory notes to individuals that denote a certain amount of gold value. Then we decided to take all of this into huge accounting ledgers that tracked every transaction so that we could be sure that no fraud was taking place and that, if gold was stolen from a bank, we still had a record of what people were 'owed' through these slips of paper.

Then we took it online, and put these ledgers into complicated algorithms, servers and spreadsheets held and managed by institutions, hedge funds, private equity managers, and people like me that make up our financial institutions. But underneath all of this there remains the same assertion that gold is valuable. To challenge this is to challenge the entire establishment, and that is what we are seeing playing out at the moment. This is a symptom of the crisis of capitalism.

THE DEMOCRATIZATION OF FINANCE

If we could re-decide what is 'valuable', and live our lives as if it were valuable, then new wealth would be created out of thin air. Cryptocurrency allows the disenfranchised generation that cannot buy houses, or pay off their parents' mortgage, or settle their student loans, or afford their rent, bills and tax, to legitimately create new value in the world and be the first to hold on to it and see it grow at the speed and volume that was seen by previous generations. To criticize and patronize a generation for innovation like this, for being at the vanguard of something, is mightily hypocritical. This is the kind of behaviour that alienates rather than unites; and it is also unhelpful because this is a moment that could benefit from some Boomer hindsight.

The suggestion that the turmoil of the crypto markets threatens to undermine the whole crypto edifice is seen as a fond imagination of an older generation. Regulated or not, debunked by pundits of stability or not, whether it is a currency as traditionally understood or not, crypto is here to stay. Probably in a form very different from what it is now but still with Zennials trying to figure the way ahead for their digital method of exchange even if Boomers reject it as a fiat currency (i.e. government-backed legal tender) or anything like it. In many ways we have been here before. The early days of the internet created just as much debate.

Elon Musk, the great Millennial prophet of cryptocurrency, understands this. There was a moment in Musk's famous appearance on the American hit show *Saturday Night Live* that was striking. In a joke interview sketch, Elon was being questioned by a fake news reporter on cryptocurrency.

The interviewer asked: 'So what actually is Dogecoin?' (Dogecoin is another alternative cryptocurrency that has previously seen skyrocketing growth due to Elon Musk championing it so voraciously.)

To which Musk replied: 'Well, they are a type of digital money not controlled by a central government that is decentralized and kept secure using blockchain technology.'

The interviewer, clearly not understanding, went on to ask, 'For instance, here's a dollar, it's real ... so what is Dogecoin?!'

Elon responded with a cheeky: 'About as real as that dollar.'

The joke clearly went over the top of most of the viewers' heads based on the live studio audience's subdued response, but this answer cuts to the heart of the cryptocurrency movement. Any currency only holds value insofar as all of us agree that it holds value. It becomes 'real' because we, collectively through central banks and governments, say it is 'real'. As soon as that comes into doubt the foundations become incredibly shaky.

This is the outcome of the discontent felt by the Zennial generation and it is a real threat to the status quo in capitalism. The generational inequality they feel in their bank balances is pushing them to question and challenge the most fundamental way we hold wealth, determine value and spend money.

And it is money, it is capital, that is at the basis of the transfer about to occur. So we need to work together to establish how best to handle the transfer of it. We need to work together to understand that finance is changing, that more people want, and more people can get, a piece of the pie. Because the ways into the world of finance have changed. The way that things used to work on Wall Street and in the City is not the way they work now. As well as the more complex areas of crypto, it is now simply easier to get yourself a stake in the stock market. You don't even need to be a 'laptop nomad', you can simply be a 'smartphone nomad'.

Investing apps abound that specifically target Zennials and untraditional investors. On the London Underground recently I spotted an advert for Revolut, a British fintech company, positioning themselves as 'your way into stock trading from £1'. The advert continued: 'Your way into stock trading without looking a certain way, going to an elite school, knowing the right people, wearing a fancy suit, or having a family crest. All you need is a phone.' This democratization of finance, opening it up to anyone with a phone, is going to change capitalism forever.

The London-based investment app Shares is another good example. Since its creation barely a year ago, it has received investment to the tune of $90 million, including from the Peter Thiel-founded Valar Ventures. Its users are almost exclusively Zennials, with 66 per cent being Gen Z and 26 per cent Millennials.[16] It is not difficult to see why.

Shares is incredibly approachable and accessible, providing access, like Revolut, to hundreds of stocks – including Apple, Disney, Alphabet, Tesla – from just £1. Its whole ethos is focused on collaboration. 'Money Moves with Mates' announces its homepage. 'Shares is the investment app where friends invest and build strategies together', it continues. A little further down: 'Investing doesn't have to be boring.' This is a world away from traditional investing. And it is bringing in new first-time investors in their droves. When it went live in the UK in May 2022, it attracted more than 150,000 new users in two months.[17]

James Fitzgerald, a partner at Valar Ventures, said of the Shares funding that it 'was an opportunity for us to invest in an innovative social trading company that challenges the status quo of traditional retail investing'.

There it is again. 'Challenging the status quo.' That is what this is all about. The status quo is being challenged. Scratch that. The status quo is over, a new one is being rewritten. But we must manage that change successfully or else capitalism dies.

Interestingly, this new type of investing is making some institutions nervous, and not without cause. In November 2022, the UK's Financial Conduct Authority issued a warning against 'gamification' in stock-trading apps, which included features like 'sending frequent notifications with the latest market news, and providing consumers with in-app points, badges and celebratory messages for making trades'. The FCA warned that 'some [consumers] appear to exhibit behaviours similar to problem-gambling' and said they had 'found that consumers using apps with these kinds of features were more likely to invest in products beyond their risk appetite'.[18] This is a genuine concern and one that Zennials would do well to heed. They are set to inherit the financial world and must treat that responsibility in a grown-up way. Investment should not be an impulsive activity; it requires thoughtful, analytical input. Dare I say it again, it requires Boomer hindsight as well as Zennial insight.

ZENNIALS MISINTERPRETED

It has become quite clear how significant the digital age has been in driving the seismic changes we have felt in these past decades as well as its role, for better or for worse, in the fractures that exist between different cohorts. It has also become clear how important the failure of key leaders and institutions has been in eroding the trust of younger generations.

One of the deepest shifts I have recognized in the younger generation is the rejection of the kind of radical individualism that defined my own. This might not come intuitively to many of us, particularly when Zennials are so often (and unfairly) described as the most narcissistic generation to have existed. In fact, in 2017, Rabbi Jonathan Sacks – one of the most courageous thinkers and communicators on moral issues of our time – argued that we have undergone a 'cultural climate change' from 'We to I' in the West particularly among the Millennial and Gen Z generations. He maintained that we have de-prioritized the needs of our wider community for the sake of our self-interest. We have put self-actualization (fulfilling my potential) above meaningfully contributing to our community. Family loyalty has taken a back seat while being 'true to yourself' has taken the wheel. We think primarily in terms of what 'I can get out of life' rather than what 'I can give to the world'.

I hugely respected Jonathan, whose books I read eagerly and whom I met on several occasions. The world is a sadder place for his passing. But I believe his is a most unfair assessment of the youth today. If anything, I think the accusation of 'We to I' applies more to my generation than Gen Z. In fact, I remember in the 1970s, people accused us, the Boomers, of being the 'Me Generation'. Sociologist Tom Wolfe, for example, wrote an essay on it in 1976 for the *New York* magazine – 'The "ME" generation and the third great awakening'. In it, he wrote:

> The new alchemical dream is: changing one's personality – remaking, remodeling, elevating, and polishing one's very self ... and observing, studying, and doting on it. (Me!) This had always been an aristocratic luxury, confined throughout most of history to the life of the courts, since

only the very wealthiest classes had the free time and the surplus income to dwell upon this sweetest and vainest of pastimes. It smacked so much of vanity, in fact, that the noble folk involved in it always took care to call it quite something else.

Does this sound familiar? That's because it is. These are precisely the same accusations we hear about young people today. If it is true that Millennials and Gen Z are the most self-centred generation in the world, we know where they learned it from. But, I don't think that is true. In actuality, I see them straining and pushing forwards to desperately move beyond the reductive, individualistic way of seeing the world. I see a new generation grappling with the big questions. I see them recognizing that our modern approaches to society have been missing something. I see them moving away from the 'I' and clutching for the 'WE'. They want a way to work together better.

I believe that Zennials have the potential to be a threshold generation who long for community and cooperation and insist on challenging the indulgences and blind spots of the previous ones. I believe they have the potential to carve out a more connected, more collaborative and more compassionate world in the coming decades. And I also believe they will only take up that mantle in the context of deep generational reconciliation, healing and collaboration. This is a possible future.

Does this sound too optimistic? Is this giving too much credit to the generation that is blamed for political polarization and the rise of the alt-right or the woke-left? Those who are the 'selfie' generation who need to be peeled from their smartphones to smell the roses? The ungrateful ones who can't hold down a job? No. I don't believe it's fanciful and I think we do them a great disservice to continue down this thinking. Indeed, it is a danger to our future to continue doing so.

To be quite honest, as I look at the practices of my industry and generation both in the home and in the workplace, I see in them the seeds of their own downfall amid the great good that was achieved. Similarly, as I look forward to the young generation that are taking their place, I don't see an ungrateful, ruinous generation destroying everything wonderful that we created. The stage was already set for fracture – they simply inherited it. They are looking to an uncharted, chaotic future and trying to identify and implement a solution.

THE NEED FOR A GUIDING HAND

All that is to say, however, the Zennials aren't without fault either. Guilt is not absolved simply by bad circumstances. It can't be ignored that what we've seen happen socially, good and bad, in the 2010s and 2020s has been driven primarily by young people. For anything to happen, you need the 'intention', the 'idea', and the 'implementation'. Zennials are filled with good intentions but more often than not, the ideas are untempered, and the implementation unrealistic. And we all know what's at the end of the road marked only by good intentions. This is why I am writing this book, to be as practical as possible, to help us find purpose in the day to day within this changing world.

I attended the annual meeting of the World Economic Forum in Davos for nearly 20 years. It is supposed to be the place where leading industrialists and financiers have the opportunity to meet politicians and also influential members in the voluntary sector. I've been there rubbing shoulders with

Bono, Mick Jagger and other luminaries, including captains of industry, finance and politics.

But I was not there in 2019 when Dutch historian and author Rutger Bregman – a Millennial – literally attacked the entire foundation of the conference with the claims that this global establishment, largely made up of an older generation, was ignoring the crisis facing the next generation. He had a plea for a new consensus based on his book *Utopia for Realists*, arguing for a universal basic income (UBI): a universal benefit to be spread as a basic income for all people, wherever they are, to be funded, largely, by increased taxation. He railed against the failure of Davos to attack tax havens and, in particular, its failure to talk about taxation. 'Nobody raises the issue of tax avoidance and the rich not paying their share,' he said at a panel on inequality organized by *Time* magazine. He saw the rest of the talk at the conference as merely being 'bullshit'.

The importance of what he was saying indicated to me the crisis in capitalism.

The irritation that prompted his simplistic answer of increased taxation and greater distribution of the pie without giving any credence to creating a wider, or bigger, pie is one of the fissures in capitalism. In a famous line he said that he felt like he was attending a firefighters conference and 'no one's allowed to talk about water'. He was dismissive of what he called 'stupid philanthropy schemes' and insisted taxes were all that mattered. In the wake of his headline-grabbing Davos moment, he was even invited onto Fox News by Tucker Carlson. The interview was terminated abruptly and prematurely – with Carlson labelling Bregman a 'moron' in an expletive-filled rebuttal – after the Dutchman had accused him of being a 'millionaire funded by billionaires'. The segment never aired on Fox.

It is worth considering the underlying philosophical point that Bregman was makes. His second book, called *Humankind: A Hopeful History*, shows that he is prepared to challenge an orthodoxy that underlies the capitalist system: that humankind is inherently selfish. Bregman argues that this is not the case. He believes humankind to be altruistic and not defined by selfishness. He says one should look to a much wider understanding of human nature in which cooperation and altruism are the governing instincts of humankind. He cites the way in which, during the peak of the Covid crisis, so many people came out in cooperative ventures – working with neighbours, delivering food and medicine – as an example of this new altruism.

ALTRUISM OR SELFISHNESS?

This is a fundamental point at which Boomers and Zennials diverge and one that has major implications for the future of capitalism. We have a Boomer generation that has experience of the defectiveness of human beings. And there is a split between this understanding of centuries of belief that life is nasty, brutish and short, and that the workplace is a tough place because of the prevalence of such degrees of personal achievement and self-interest. Whereas Bregman would argue that there is a new generation for whom the redefinition of humankind is right in front of us: humanity is, in its essence, looking for the good, for the positive, for close relationships, for altruism. But the Ukraine war has halted this thinking in its tracks.

Here is the hindsight and insight argument that we need to be able to understand. Although the desires of altruism are there, the capitalist system needs to embody both – doing good and doing well – but cannot accept that there is a base goodness, as the evidence of humankind is such that this must, at the very least, be qualified.

We need to work within a tension between the under-standing, championed by more conservative philosophers, that at its root humankind is self-satisfied and will always seek its own interests but can be persuaded towards the altruism that Bregman advocates. It is essential for capital markets to be able to enter into this debate, otherwise the inevitable increase in taxation will come at the expense of the incentive-based proliferation of value-added activity. If there is to be a UBI, it can only be when there is significant global growth to be able to pay for it. But one cannot just dismiss UBI as being a fantasy of a generation, as the change in technology, the changes in the workplace, will mean that a much more serious opportunity now exists to examine whether, consistent with the capitalist system, it is feasible to assume that there would be a basic human income payable without causing the entire market economy to collapse.

NOT A NEW SOCIALISM

This is a prime example of the crisis – or opportunity, depending on how you look at it – facing capitalism. What we have at present is a system outdated, not recognizable or attractive to the generation set to control the narrative as we move forward in the twenty-first century. And the danger facing us if Zennials' insights are imposed without the hindsight of the Boomer is that a new socialism could take hold that would threaten the fundamentals of an incentive-based market. It is a possibility that intergenerational tensions reach an irreversible tipping point and the entire economic project could collapse. This is why Boomers and Zennials need to work together to change the current system for the better rather than destroy it completely.

We need to avoid the scenario that leads us into a world where we end up with a facsimile of Chinese president Xi Jinping's 'common prosperity' policy. The concept of common prosperity is nothing new in China, the first mention of the idea coming in the 1950s with Chairman Mao, then repeated by Deng Xiaoping in the 1980s. The new version has surface-level attraction, especially to a Zennial generation who are far more sympathetic to socialist ideas than their parents. Xi himself has said on the aims of the policy: 'We will first make the pie bigger and then divide it properly through reasonable institutional arrangements. As a rising tide lifts all boats, everyone will get a fair share from development, and development gains will benefit all our people in a more substantial and equitable way.' In theory, an idea that many could get behind.

But as so often with ideologies, it dissolves when it comes into contact with air. Its current practical applications are nil because nobody really knows what it is. And that vagueness is intentional. As David Moser, an associate professor at Beijing's Capital Normal University, has pointed out, it mirrors the anti-corruption drive started by Xi in 2012. That scheme did not see new laws and regulations introduced to ensure transparency and accountability. Instead it utilized the ancient Chinese tactic of 'kill a chicken to scare the monkeys', with 1.5 million officials made examples of to send a clear message to others that corruption would no longer be tolerated. Hardly a comprehensive or sustainable strategy.[19] When Xi uses metaphor and rhetoric to describe his new policy, rather than specifics, he is simply continuing in that tradition.

The Chinese Communist Party has promised that common prosperity will not mean 'killing the rich to help the poor',[20] but it is unquestionably a socialist policy – not a huge surprise in a communist country. What it has already meant in practice is an increase in regulation that has wiped hundreds of billions off the market value of China's leading tech companies.[21] It is a policy that has rattled investors due to its potential for disincentivizing profit and growth, exactly the opposite of what any sane capitalist would want.

The London School of Economics and Political Science put out a 20-page paper in April 2022 by Dr Xin Sun entitled 'Decoding China's "Common Prosperity" Drive'. Having economic strategies and policies that need to be 'decoded' is exactly what I know we need to avoid. As is having economic policies that stunt growth, resist experimentation and fail to reward successful innovation. It is not revolution we are after. It is not throwing out the whole system because it is not functioning perfectly. Reformation and renewal are what is needed. The resources and the will are there to make a better system for all to benefit from. But pursuing this path towards a renewed capitalism is a tall order, fraught with danger and challenges.

THE CHALLENGES AHEAD

First, the rapid acceleration of new technological development brings challenges. These innovations that have brought unprecedented connection between people have also resulted in isolation, disconnection and echo chambers that have birthed movements threatening capitalism's existence. In addition, the rapid technological acceleration in AI, space travel and quantum computing means so much is unknown.

I am actually an investor in a company that is aiming 'to accelerate quantum computing and use its power to positively transform the world. By applying the laws of quantum physics to computing, we will achieve unprecedented breakthroughs in drug discovery, healthcare, materials science, cybersecurity, energy transformation and climate change.'[22] These are lofty and extraordinarily ambitious goals, which, if met, will be genuinely transformational to the world. However, the attitude with which I treat the potential benefits of quantum computing, and how Zennials do, differs hugely. I and my contemporaries have what I believe to be a necessary scepticism – some might call it fear – towards the claims of what new technologies can do. Zennials do not have this fear and can sometimes drink the Kool-Aid all too quickly. (Elizabeth Holmes's Theranos comes to mind here.) I invest in these projects, of course, because I believe in them and am excited by their possibilities. But I also bring that scepticism, that hindsight, that can help temper the worst of Zennial instincts when it comes to tech. We must not forget that even the most established tech industry players are still in their infancy compared to the likes of centuries-old physical infrastructures like roads and railways. But digital infrastructure is here to stay even though it's in its infancy.

Second, if the capitalist system is to be renewed – which I believe it must – trust in institutions and the flow of information must be restored. A market cannot function without the availability of reasonably trustworthy information for all parties. In a time when we have more people directly engaging with the markets than ever before, and even more information being churned out and disseminated, this will not be easy.

For an efficient capital market to function, truth needs to be at its heart. The prevailing climate of fake truth, subjective facts and personalized morality is problematic. This 'Wikimorality', where anyone can advance a view without any objective checking, will have to be abandoned. Nimble regulators will need to keep the financial market trustworthy to all participants, especially the new Zennial investors.

As well as fake truth and personal morality, there are worrying threats to freedom and financial decision making because of the way in which algorithms now govern our digital lives. Algorithms increasingly dictate our decisions and the information to which we have access. Algo-ethics will need to be assessed with cool detachment to ensure that our choices are genuinely driven by reasonable freedom rather than at the behest of an unseen, usually commercially-driven corporate hand.

The crypto trend is another area of challenge. A deep distrust of fiat currency has led to the massive Zennial-driven crypto growth. Currently there are 295 million users.[23] It will not be long until there are over a billion.

As already discussed, cryptocurrency has emerged as a direct challenge to the centralization and distrust of currencies debased by decades of quantitative easing. Crypto has grown faster than any other technology sector. It is not a reflection of a purposeless, or greed-driven intervention to unsettle the capital markets; and it's not a scam. However, the revolution is volatile – as has been seen recently – and is supercharged with discontent and internet meme culture. Regulators must seek to truly understand the fundamental shift in the economic zeitgeist driven by the Zennials, rather than scramble to outsmart them with efforts like 'Britcoin' (the official UK central-bank-driven cryptocurrency). They have come late to the crypto party and will need to justify their crypto initiatives against the background of a sceptical user base.

Finally, a renewed capitalism is threatened by those who seek to deconstruct without rebuilding. Despite this trend towards cooperation and collaboration, many Zennials are isolated and socially disconnected, living in tribal, homogenized silos of like-minded fellow travellers. This is a recipe for extremism, which threatens the capitalist system itself; connected isolation is not a basis on which to build a healthy economy. Many of these Zennials believe that capitalism is inherently morally bankrupt. For some of them at the extreme end, the only way forward is to raze it to the ground and replace it with a quasi-Marxism or de-centralized anarchism. This undermines the good and valuable work of the Zennial entrepreneurs who are pushing for positive change in the capital markets. Capitalism is under a huge amount of pressure and there is a risk that it will be demolished in all-out conflict.

I remember being interviewed in 2018 by the *Financial Times*, having just been appointed co-chairman of a new global fund management company. I commented that 'we wish to be a merchant bank for the Millennials'. At the time, seasoned colleagues in the industry smiled benignly at this apparently altruistic but impractical thought.

They smile less often now.

The global economy will face some of its greatest challenges in the next 40 years and it will be on the shoulders of the Zennials. The future is uncharted and chaotic, and it will become more disruptive, not less, as the technology industry continues to mature and drastically change how we live our lives. In light of these challenges, it is vital that we wisely navigate the road towards a new capitalism, together. For generational tension to be healed, we need the hindsight of the Boomer and the insight of the Zennial to be drawn together and harmonized in an intergenerational education project; iron sharpens iron after all. Generational conflict and infighting will be our downfall. Constant belittling of the Zennials or demonization of the Boomer will just end in catastrophe.

But a union of the two will take us through the current period of flux and into an era where we can be hopeful, motivated and excited for both the future of our planet and the future of capitalism. I absolutely believe that the two groups working together can create something new and exciting that re-establishes the fundamentals of capitalism in a way that will be satisfactory in decades and centuries to come. Wisdom is the key to achieving this success. I use wisdom advisedly here because it is different from knowledge. Knowledge is almost a given in the twenty-first century. If you don't know something, you Google it. And further in the future the actual action of Googling will be obsolete, the possibilities of machine learning and AI being what they are.

But you cannot Google wisdom. Nor could you describe Google as wise. Because wisdom is about judgement, and it is the judgement calls that have been wrong in the past couple of decades, and that could be wrong in the future couple of decades, that could lead us into an irretrievable situation. But we are not there yet. For the moment as a society we are knowledge long and wisdom short.

To stress again, the way we make the wise choices is by collaborating and communicating; by understanding that it is the fusion of the hindsight of the Boomer – the experience, the knowledge, the understanding – and the insight of the Zennial – the skills, the ambitions, the principles – that can create a fundamentally noble and beautiful vision for humanity in which the market economy can thrive for the benefit of all.

3

THE TECH FISSURE

The most obvious distinction between Boomers and Zennials is in technology. Tech, for Zennials, is the great enabler. Meanwhile, for Boomers, tech is the means by which the status quo is being broken and the power is being taken away from those who have held it up until now. Tech helps to democratize more than finance – although its role in changing the face of finance will be huge. It is able to empower groups that have previously never had a voice and connect people from across the globe. It also, though, has the ability to isolate. Crucially, the group that is able to use tech most effectively will have the ability to enact more rapid change than we've ever seen before. When it comes to the generations, there is only one winner here.

NATIVES AND IMMIGRANTS

Way back in 2001, the American writer Marc Prensky posited the idea that the rapid dissemination of digital technology in the last decades of the twentieth century, and the fact that the youth of the day had 'spent their entire lives surrounded by and using computers, video games, digital music players, video cams, cell phones, and all the other toys and tools of the digital age', meant that young people in 2001 (Millennials) 'think and process information fundamentally differently from their predecessors'.[1]

That's remarkable prescience on the part of Prensky given that here I am – and I am not alone – more than two decades later trying to unpick that exact phenomena. Perhaps his major contribution to the ongoing discussion, though, was to popularize the term *digital natives* to describe this new generation forged in the emerging – as it was then – digital landscape. Less widely used now but equally evocative was his use of *digital immigrants* to describe the older generations. Or in his words: 'Those of us who were not born into the digital world but have, at some later point in our lives, become fascinated by and adopted many or most aspects of the new technology.'

These are brilliantly useful terms to use in describing the different ways in which Zennials and Boomers interact with and perceive the world. But the oddity for those like me, the *digital immigrants*, is that it was our world first. Shouldn't it be the Zennials that are the immigrants, the new arrivals? It certainly doesn't feel like it. And if Prensky was noticing the differences between natives and immigrants in 2001, think about the technological developments that have happened since.

It's difficult to believe, but the iPhone has only been part of our world since 2007. Similarly, apps like Instagram, WhatsApp and Twitter, that have toppled governments and shifted the geo-political scales, couldn't even legally buy a drink if they were human beings. Technology has always moved to reshape the world, but very few technologies have done so at such a rapid pace.

The Gutenberg Press was invented in 1440; it was 15 years later that the first ever full book, *The Gutenberg Bible*, was printed in 1455. 'The Facebook' was first created in 2004;

within 15 years *it* was in the hands of 2.3 billion people, more than a quarter of the world population, and has substantially shifted (some could argue broken) the democratic systems of two major powers in the Western world in the shape of the Brexit referendum and the 2016 US election. The only technology comparable to this kind of speed and disruption was the discovery of nuclear energy. When the Jewish scientist, Leo Szilard, fled the Nazi regime, he introduced the world to the idea of splitting the atom in his 1934 paper on nuclear chain reactions. Eleven years later, after a furious technological race between the US and the Nazi Party, Oppenheimer's bomb changed the nature of war forever.

We do not think of our current position in those terms. But the changes that have taken place philosophically, sociologically and technologically over the last two decades are analogous to that of the Manhattan project – the US government research project that produced the first atomic bombs. It will, and has, changed the world forever, and I believe for the better. And it is also just getting started.

THE REACH OF TECH

The twenty-first century has truly been the 'connected century'. Several different technological innovations have conspired to bring us to the point we are now. Personal computers and smartphones became accessible to the masses in the last 30 years, the internet brought a level of connectivity between those personal devices in a way previously thought impossible, and new social media and apps were developed to harness that connectivity and democratize its tools to every person walking down the street. Without this convergence of hardware, software and services, we would not be where we are today – and it is this convergence of technological leaps that we often call the 'digital revolution'. This revolution is perhaps the most impactful and meaningful development in human technology since the printing press.

It has changed the way we communicate, work, socialize, interact and self-identify. We are no longer restricted to our own bodies, the material facts of our own lives. It has made permeable dividing walls that had historically kept individuals and communities apart – geographic location, national borders, language barriers, knowledge and information access. No longer do you have to walk to the library in the next town over to find a book or wait for a translation of an article to be released in your country. A quick Google search and a click of the 'Google Translate' button will give you access to more information than you could ever consume in a million lifetimes (or so).

It has been the great democratizer, making information, platforms, creative tools and expertise available to anyone with an internet connection.

Take a moment to consider what it would take to communicate your thoughts to just 300 people in the 1950s, 1960s or even 1970s. You'd need to be a vicar, a journalist, a politician, or you would need to go and stand on Speaker's Corner in Hyde Park in London to shout your message to the masses – although you'd have no guarantee they'd listen.

Today, 300 followers is a very modest Twitter or Instagram following. Very modest indeed. In *The Social Network*, David Fincher's 2010 film about the origins of Facebook, a character marvels at the fact that 650 Harvard students signed up to the site on the first day with the immortal line: 'If I was a drug dealer I couldn't give free drugs to 650 people in one day.' In 2023, Portuguese footballer Cristiano Ronaldo's is the most popular account on Instagram with 581 million followers, ahead of fellow footballing icon Lionel Messi (457 million) and American actress Selena Gomez (412 million). All three are, unsurprisingly, Zennials.

The reach of technology is truly staggering. It has felt as though the last decade has been one of exponential connection, allowing remarkable achievements previously thought unimaginable.

THE TWO SIDES OF TECH

We often lament the fact that Zennials are 'addicted to their phones'. True, young people use technology for mindless entertainment, but they do also to stay informed about world events, to research topics they are interested in, to amplify voices that otherwise might go unheard, and to create new systems and processes that benefit society – all of which help to establish a global community unlike anything we've ever seen before. There is common ground globally as connectivity links generations across the globe. This extraordinary level of connection was driven home to me on a recent visit to Chad in Africa, one of the poorest nations in the world. There is a substantial nomad tradition there and tribespeople move around on camels, donkeys and sometimes horses. We attended a market which drew thousands of traders to sell their wares and to bargain in the livestock market. It was reminiscent of biblical times. Literacy was useful only numerically to bargain in the livestock market. Education is very low. But what was remarkable was that almost everyone, even the oldest and most wizened, had smartphones. Battered by weather and desert conditions, it was as if they had escaped the whole age of education and had leapfrogged into the modern era. Camel traders and itinerant herders united in the use of their iPhones. Our capability to do good actually increases because we are more connected. There are plenty of stories on the internet connecting strangers for simple acts of kindness – this was most evident at the height of lockdown in the UK during the coronavirus pandemic. Who can forget Captain Tom Moore, the Second World War veteran, who had the humble goal of raising £1,000 by walking laps of his garden in the run-up to his 100th birthday? Who would have thought he would raise an extraordinary crowdfunded £32.79 million for the NHS by the time his birthday rolled around?

The UK press and BBC went wild for this story; social media was alight with hope and encouragement; and none of it would have been possible without digital connection. Connectivity has the power to mobilize ordinary people in extraordinary ways. This is a small example, but we can blow it up to the largest scale. How do we expect to address any of the hyper-complex issues of our world like the climate crisis if we cannot leverage the ability to harness the 4.5 billion people with an internet connection in the world? How do we send the message out? How do we organize a movement of that size? How do we connect?

However, this has not come without its serious costs. While it has been a century of exponential connection, it has sometimes felt like the century of 'disconnection' where this unfettered technological drive has led to personal dislocation and an epidemic of isolation. Like all technological leaps, the shadow is as dark as the light is bright. Digital connectivity has been a very powerful force for good and change in the world. However, in the years preceding the third decade of the twenty-first century we have seen more images and stories of dystopian technological terrors than a beautiful vision of the future.

The stories we tell ourselves about how digital media will shape our future have been deeply cynical and tragic. Tristan

Harris, the American digital ethicist made famous by the documentary *The Social Dilemma* and his work on exposing Big Tech's attention economy talks about how we are on a trajectory of societal collapse if we do not shift course right now. He is convinced that the attention-advertising economy of social media giants will continue to erode our ability to take part in civil discourse as we continue to be insulated in our socio-political echo chambers.

Thoughts, pictures, memes and tropes are communicated instantly and, in many cases, thoughtlessly. Little time is taken over publishing them and the brevity of tweets encourages the tremendously toxic Twitter storms of our times. I'm not saying that the 'good old days' was an era of deep thought and reflection, but the mediums available, like speeches, letters and printed formats, slowed the speed of connection and therefore encouraged consequential thoughts and safeguarded the most reactive verbal stabs. What I am saying, also, is that the epidemic of quick-response embedded in social media directly affects the way in which a generation will make investment and business decisions. High-frequency trading is a programmatic way of dealing, but is very different from impulse trading, which is the pervasive habit of rapid response that social media encourages.

Algorithms push us further away from the centre and create tribal groups on every side that vilify the other. Similarly, we hear stories of the 'Chinese Social Credit Score' system where the government issues 'points' to their citizens for good behaviour, rewarding those with lots of points and punishing those with less. Rewards can range from discounts in shops and utility bills, while punishments can range from travel bans, exclusion from certain schools, and reportedly, incarceration. It's all alarmingly reminiscent of the strikingly prescient dystopian anthology series, *Black Mirror*.

When I was growing up, the fear was nuclear annihilation, where human civilization is wiped out in a blinding flash. Today, the fear seems palpably to be that of societal disintegration, where human civilization is torturously reduced year after year by totalitarian states or our own inability to get along. These are the stories we tell ourselves today. This is both the Orwellian nightmare of *1984* and the Huxleyan stupor of *Brave New World*. Like Big Brother, tech companies and governments are engaged in mass surveillance capitalism, able to shape the inner lives and emotions of the individual, and stamping out anything unsavoury. Meanwhile, we are being sedated with pleasurable distractions found on the internet and being exposed to only the things that we like and agree with. Just like Huxley's nightmarish vision, you don't need authoritative power to control a population, you just need to distract it to submission. Markets, to be efficient, need independent judgements from investors. The herd instinct encouraged by the prevailing social trends inevitably lead to financial disasters, as the dot-com bubble and the current tech rout clearly demonstrate.

Whether this is overly catastrophizing or not, one thing is sure: the way we do human relationships has changed forever. And with it has come a potentially catastrophic undermining of the very foundation of capitalism. This accelerated change has created deep fractures in our human relationships. While we are more connected than ever before across borders and communities, our closer, personal connections have been fractured. This has played a huge role in the intergenerational wedge that we have already discussed, which is at the heart of the crisis in capitalism we analysed in the previous chapter.

FUNCTIONAL VS ONTOLOGICAL

I remember when the first desktop computer appeared in our office. The great unique selling point was the improvement in productivity (oh the irony!). The computer used to be seen simply as the great improver of efficiency to make workloads easier and to improve output – it was simply a tool. It might seem baffling to people today, but there was a time when spreadsheets were sheets of paper spread out on a real wooden table. That might sound romantic and rustic, but it was the bane of my life before we could create massive tabulations on our desktop computer – that was a tool that made my job infinitely easier. Since then, however, the posture towards technology has shifted – it remains a tool but it is also something so much more.

What I find remarkable when I mentor young people is that the relationship between the Zennial generation and their smart devices is an ontological one and not simply a functional one. What I mean by this is that the relationship is one where technology makes up something of 'who I am as a person' beyond simply 'how I can use technology'. Modern devices are now an essential part of the being, purpose and life itself of a generation. Our smart devices are an extension of ourselves – this is what I mean when I say we have an ontological relationship with them. They are no longer external things but have become a core part of our identities. We are the devices and the devices are now us. Encoded in these devices and the various accounts we own is the whole defining picture of a person's life. If you think this is taking something too far, imagine handing over your unlocked smartphone to even your closest friend – how long until the anxiety would mount to unbearable heights that you cannot help but ask for it back? It'd be like allowing them into your thoughts.

Never before has one piece of technology aggregated so much of ourselves: our memories are stored in the form of thousands of photo snapshots; our curiosities and questions are laid out like a map in our browser history; and our relationships, commitments and networks are on display in our messages, who we follow, and what we publish. And these devices are now the cornerstone of the market-based economy.

CLICKTIVISM AND THE POWER OF THE

It's this quality of digital connectivity that makes the internet different from previous technological advancements, and what enables it to be a driving force for unifying the generations, an absolute necessity if we are to develop a sustainable capitalism. If these new devices and platforms did not represent our identities in a meaningful way, solidarity shown through them would be meaningless. And corporations would be able to ignore the rallying cries of many when it comes to demands for social equality in the workplace. But they can't. Steve Jobs was quite clear and prescient. He never intended Apple's products to merely be functional communications tools. The iPhone was and has become a powerful instrument of empowerment.

I used to be very disparaging of what people call 'Clicktivism' – this idea that people can now support causes and justice issues with no cost to themselves simply by sharing an image or liking a post. What I've come to realize, however, is that there was a deep fallacy in my thinking. The fact is that it *does* cost something to participate in public discourse in the digital world just as much as it costs to participate in the public discourse in the physical world. It costs Zennials a share of their voice, a share of their platform, and a share of their identity that is tied up in the digital world. Some say that sharing hashtags can't change the world ... #BlackLivesMatter would disagree.

Many readers will know this story. In 2013 in Florida, a neighbourhood watch coordinator named George Zimmerman was acquitted in court after he followed and fatally shot an unarmed black teenager. Around the same time, three young women named Alicia Garza, Patrisse Cullors and Opal Tometi met through a national community organizing programme named BOLD ('Black Organizing for Leadership and Dignity'). Upon hearing of Zimmerman's acquittal, Garza wrote a Facebook post titled 'A Love Note to Black People', which included the line 'Our Lives Matter, Black Lives Matter'. Cullors commented #BlackLivesMatter, Tometi added her support, and the hashtag began to spread.

The teenager's name was Trayvon Martin, and his death was the birth of a movement. The advent of social media has doubtless transformed the face of activism, but any protest made to stick doesn't just exist online. Black Lives Matter left the digital world for street demonstrations in 2014, when the deaths of two more African Americans at the hands of law enforcement made headlines: Michael Brown in Ferguson, Missouri, and Eric Garner in New York City. In August, more than 500 online members of Black Lives Matter participated in a 'Black Lives Matter Freedom Ride' to Ferguson, where multiple other groups had also descended. BLM's non-violent protest was highly coordinated, and they began to gather national recognition (and critique). Continuing to coordinate through social media platforms, BLM has since provided a physical and virtual campaign in response to numerous other African American deaths as a result of police involvement. In 2014, the American Dialect Society chose #BlackLivesMatter as their 'word of the year'. The names of Garza, Cullors and Tometi have largely been forgotten by the press, but their hashtag has grown into over 40 local chapters across the United States and has inspired other related hashtags (see #BlackGirlsMatter, #BlackQueerLivesMatter, and even the critique hashtag #BlueLivesMatter, referring to police deaths) and international groups, including in Australia, Canada, the United Kingdom and Israel. Though decentralized in structure, their locally run protests have often emphasized partnership with other marginalized peoples or have posed critiques of 'anti-blackness' present in other communities. In May 2020, the movement reached a boiling point after the death of George Floyd was broadcast on video across social media, sparking protests across the world amid the frenzy of the coronavirus pandemic and its related lockdowns.

BLM, in particular, is a movement where the distinction between physical and digital, local and global, is razor thin. The digital universe has been transformed just as much as the physical world, and new online content that seeks to inform people about the issues have been just as important as the physical protests. Arguably, sharing a #BLM video is just as activist as taking to the streets. The mass social sharing of one man's story in these online platforms did what no traditional publisher or PR group could ever do: capture the attention of the whole world. Whether or not you believe that these protests are a constructive or a destructive force, it is impossible to deny the power of connection in taking what is local, and making it something global.

Black Lives Matter did not need a magnanimous individual to muster a social, global army; it was the actions of ordinary individuals and their connected networks working together that pushed it to become a global movement. It took what are localized issues, and blew them up into a global movement in a matter of months, if not moments. This is one of the defining characteristics of the digital revolution that makes it so powerful. There is no 'bar of entry' or a 'ceiling of reach' – everything is fair game, and everything has the potential to explode. However, this relationship of the local and the global is not a two-way street.

BLM is not just a social phenomenon. Its effects are evident throughout the business world. No boardroom in any part of the globe has been able to avoid addressing the issue of race. If not in the specific terms of the BLM movement then in the way in which diversity is dealt with, monitored and encouraged in the workplace. Racial injustice was not created by BLM activists but it became one of the trigger points for the corporate world to address race in the workplace as a matter of urgency and priority. Board reviews and C-suite-level participation showed a renewed intensity in scrutinizing the performance of corporations.

There is a Boomer caution, however. Having spent my student days in South Africa in the anti-apartheid struggle, I understand the reality of racial prejudice, though I cannot imagine what it must be like to be on the receiving end. I joined the BLM march in London – probably the only banker to do so! My real dilemma was joining in a march organized by Black Lives Matter when on close inspection of their publicity it appeared that so many of the objectives spelt out were fundamentally opposed to those which I valued. It was, however, a case of joining as a co-belligerent.

I saw this as a small way of expressing solidarity not only with people of colour but also with the next generation, who were the ones turning up in their droves on the march to Parliament Square. The sadness to me was that I was in a demonstration in London 50 years after the time when I would have been in similar demonstrations on the streets of Johannesburg. I wondered how it was that, after 50 years, racial prejudice was still so endemic in our society. Had we not learned and did it take a Zennial activist group to drive the agenda to the heart of the business community? It's the #, not the hedge fund that the C-suite fear most. And the invisible hand that holds the # is in the power of the Zennial cohort.

CONNECTED ISOLATION

Digital connectivity may be very good at taking what is localized and feeding it into a global conversation. But it is not so good at taking global forces and constructively integrating them into local communities and individuals. This is where we see the fractures in our relationships. This is where the dissonance begins to resound of how we can feel so connected, yet so lonely. It is this fundamental difference that being a collective is not the same as being in a relationship or being in a community. Being connected does not mean we cannot be isolated. Many of us live in connected isolation. Mental health issues have become one of the greatest threats of our time, and a threat that needs to be dealt with at every level. Not just familial or social, but corporate. This is a boardroom issue of immense magnitude. Human Resources departments the world over will need to be prepared to deal with it effectively or risk having company profits impacted upon. Because in order to have effective productivity there needs to be relational health.

In 2018, London appointed its first Minister for Loneliness after it was discovered that up to a fifth of UK adults feel lonely most or all of the time; the figures were up at

30 per cent for young people in 2019. When asked about technology and social media, the Minister, Tracey Crouch, said that technology played a significant role in the increased isolation of individuals. The increase of remote working during Covid has meant people are increasingly atomized in their professional lives as well, and social media is giving the illusion of relational depth while not actually providing the intimacy required to sate the loneliness. A harrowing video published by *The Atlantic*[2] in 2020 featured voicemails left by young people to the Minister of Loneliness. In a rare piece of video journalism, they lifted the lid on the inner lives of these Zennials and found the toxic shadow of connection – connected isolation.

One said: 'Social media is a poison ... but it's a good poison which makes you want to carry on drinking.' Another made the prescient point that 'The more this world seems to be getting connected by the internet and social media, the more disconnected we've become.'

Another young woman talked about her experience of abject social isolation and a moment when she had been travelling on the London Underground back to the flat-share that she desperately did not want to return to because she did not like her housemates. 'It was rush hour,' she said, 'and I was standing up on the Tube and there were so many people around me. And I was just sobbing. Not one single person looked up or saw me or spoke to me just to even ask if I was okay ... not one single person. In that moment I've never felt so isolated.'

In one of the most scathing critiques of digital connectivity and social media, Sherry Turkle, author of *Alone Together: Why We Expect More from Technology and Less from Each Other*, writes that technology is seductive when what it offers meets our human vulnerabilities. And as it turns out, we are vulnerable indeed. We are lonely but fearful of intimacy. Digital connections and the sociable robot may offer the illusion of companionship without the demands of friendship. Our networked life allows us to hide from each other, even as we are tethered to each other ... We expect more from technology and less from each other.

The shadow of connected isolation is dark and long. We are in a state of globalized connection, but personal isolation. We cannot let the optimism of the connected world and technological advancement wallpaper over these deep wounds that are being left in the human psyche. It is not simply teenage angst or poor self-control, it is nothing short of violence to the soul. In many ways, it is nothing short of a captivity. And this is significantly, if not principally, expressed at work, where productivity suffers as a result.

The great irony of connected isolation is that the very tools that can mobilize hundreds of thousands of people to great effect and create communities that transcend all boundary lines are the same as those that have the potential to create a chasm of intimacy between us. This needs to be addressed by this generation or else the costs of the digital revolution will begin to outweigh the great benefits.

Don't misunderstand me however: I don't want to be another voice making noise and banging drums to tell the world how terrible and awful the digital age is and how social media is destroying our youth and our future. It does, though, concern me greatly that the tool that has brought so many people together is also the prison that causes so much social isolation and sadness. And no corporation will survive long into the future without a clear plan to address this.

At the first instance, what is encouraging is that Zennials have been quick to understand this. Even Mark Zuckerberg recognized it and the role his company had played in the atomization of society. In 2017, the company published an open letter about the desperate need to build a 'global community', and to create social infrastructure that can support the changing digital landscape. Zuckerberg writes that he wants to make this increasingly connected world resistant to atomization, saying that 'our job at Facebook is to help people make the greatest positive impact while mitigating areas where technology and social media can contribute to divisiveness and isolation'. It can be easy to roll our eyes at tech billionaires like Zuckerberg when they make these kinds of statements, and it can be rather satisfying to launch attacks at their character and say they are not doing enough. But the reality is that connected isolation is a very difficult spectre to overcome, and it is primarily not a technological problem but a human one. To overcome it, we must all be united. Not just a few of us. All of us.

As Sherry Turkle points out, social media caters to our fear of commitment and temptation to avoid vulnerability and intimacy, and fuels our need for recognition, making us act in performative and inauthentic ways. In response to some of these insights, Facebook has begun rolling out various policies in an attempt to combat this danger such as promoting various 'group' functions to encourage community building, or hiding how many 'likes' you get on Instagram to reduce the social anxiety felt by its users to maintain a certain level of 'fame'.

These are respectable first steps. However, I am sceptical as to how effective they will be. It's no good trying to Tippex over a giant crack in your wall (younger readers can Google

Tippex!). Technocratic solutions don't solve human problems. I have an intuition that it will not be a tech solution that will solve deep human, existential issues of loneliness. It will require deeply human solutions to help us overcome these. After all, loneliness and isolation is not a new phenomenon – thousands of generations of humans have existed struggling with both long before Facebook or Twitter.

DIGITAL GLOCALISM

A key tension I have noticed in many Zennials is that they at once hold a deep desire to participate in global endeavours, and at the same time, desire to truly participate in a flourishing local community. As mentioned earlier, connection is a fantastic means of participating in global issues. By and large, active global participation encourages small actions by the masses to enact massive change. In this space, the sharing of a hashtag or promoting an eco-friendly brand really do make a difference so long as they are done on scale. These are how global endeavours are tackled – small decisions at scale. The level of individual commitment and vulnerability depends on how much you want to invest.

The danger is to assume that this strategy can be imported into every area of life. In the 1980s, there was a buzzword in the business community: 'glocalism'. It was the idea that tried to deconstruct the distinction between 'global' and 'local' issues, arguing that these two domains were deeply interconnected and interdependent, and if you wanted a successful international business, you had to allow for global macro brand considerations alongside highly localized insights. Sociologist Roland Robertson stated that glocalization 'means the simultaneity – the co-presence – of both universalizing and particularizing tendencies'. How this was applied in the business world was through franchises like McDonald's and Starbucks investing huge amounts of resources to ensure that a shop in China was at once harmonized with the global brand ambition of providing American fast food as well as creating a specific localized experience. This is why if you walk into a McDonald's in the UK, you can pick up a curry sauce packet and a breakfast McMuffin, while in India you can get yourself a spicy paneer burger – but both feel distinctly McDonald's. Glocalism recognized that just because you can reach a billion people with your brand, you can't ever replace the particularities of the local. There are some things the economy of scale simply can't buy. And this is the same with digital connected isolation.

Connected isolation is not a global issue that can be fixed with small actions done en masse, like recycling. It is an issue that requires the re-cultivation of friendships, local communities, discipline and associations. It is not something that will be fixed by collective action, but one that can only be repaired by deep individual actions together. It requires daily sacrifices of our time and emotional energy into relational pursuits that will go unseen and unrecognized.

Dostoevsky wrote in *The Brothers Karamazov* that, for young people, 'the sacrifice of life [to a cause] is, perhaps, the easiest of all sacrifices in many cases, while to sacrifice, for example, five or six years of their youthful life to hard, difficult studies, to learning, in order to increase tenfold their strength to serve the very truth and the very deed that they loved and set out to accomplish – such sacrifice is quite often almost beyond the strength of many of them'.

Zennials today are zealous and fiery. They have many causes to fight for and the infinitely powerful tools to champion those causes. However, it can sometimes be easier to sacrifice our entire digital lives and social capital to this or that cause, getting caught up in the feeling that we are part of something global and magnificent, than to spend the years of youth talking with your neighbour and making friends. We must connect not only to the globe but also to our immediate locality and ourselves. We cannot subcontract our humanity. At a time when globalization is under threat and there is a retreat into the nation-state and its needs, and with global supply chains under threat, there is a populist call to reverse-engineer the Boomer decades of global expansion in favour of a more isolationist economy. The pitfalls in this reverse thrust will become obvious as trade barriers and protectionist policies take root. Globalization might have led to serious dislocation but its benefits are obvious in terms of the increase in productivity. It would be dangerous to throw these advantages out with the bathwater of isolationism.

INTRA- AND INTER-GENERATIONAL FRACTURE

Technology is the tool for change that will be used by the beneficiaries of the Great Wealth Transfer. As we have discussed, tech has huge power to be a force for good. But it is also causing fissures between and among generations. There is a fundamental difference in the way Boomers and Zennials engage with tech – one group as natives and the other as immigrants – that needs to be rationalized if it is to bring the two cohorts together. But, perhaps more significantly, there is the possible damage that tech is causing to relations within the Zennial generation.

Without a corrective, this has the potential to create a generation that loves the world but forgets its neighbours. It can create people with infinity in their pockets but a lack of love in their hearts. It can create a global people without a local home. Digital connectivity may be able to unite humanity, but it will never unite people. It 'lacks the physical gestures, facial expressions, moments of silence, body language and even the smells, the trembling of hands, the blushes and perspiration that speak to us and are a part of human communication', as Pope Francis wrote in 2020.[3]

In all the companies I have been involved in, the personal and the profitable run together. The danger is that silos of individual achievement, if unchecked, will fracture the very basis of capitalism in the corporation.

It is vital that we encourage a responsible attitude towards digital connectivity. As the borders between the digital and physical world become increasingly permeable, it will become increasingly more important that we demarcate the areas that cannot be delegated and optimized digitally. Google rightly recognizes that 'digital activities on their own are not binarily positive or negative' but are highly dependent on the effect they have on people and their communities.

Fortunately, this is already happening. As noted by Google's Digital Wellbeing report, one in four people have made changes to their technology to gain a greater sense of digital wellbeing and have begun implementing changes to their lives such as deleting certain apps, changing notification settings, and reducing time spent on certain social media apps. Like all things in life, we ought to take the posture of stewards and servants. We are stewards and servants of society rather than proprietors; we are stewards and servants also of the digital communities and profiles we are building. We can overcome the shadow of connection and maximize the benefits of all the new technologies that are shaping the world today.

But it requires a recognition that connectivity by itself cannot solve the problems of the world, and the problems of your neighbourhood. We can start by making those sacrifices that may result in us feeling estranged and on the fringes of global, exciting movements, intentionally putting ourselves in a state of FOMO, with the ultimate aim of greater connection with those beside us – balancing the scales between digital global engagement and physical local incarnation. We can start by becoming more cognizant of our connection with the natural world, which reminds us of the ancient truth that 'man is from the dust' and cannot be replaced by ephemeral 1s and 0s. No business or institution will be able to flourish without addressing these issues of connectivity, productivity and the human cost. Holding these together will be the key challenge of the digital economy in the next generation.

4

The Challenge of Individualism

We have, so far, in explaining the predicament we find ourselves in ahead of the Great Wealth Transfer, examined how and why generational tensions have reached breaking point, why capitalism needs to adapt or potentially die, and the fissures that the advancement in tech has created in our society, and why all this has implications not only for corporations around the world but for our very way of life in the future.

We are now going to look at the breakdown of communities: the collapse, across the Western world certainly, of support groups, families, societies, voluntary charity organizations, Saturday football clubs, and town halls. This is an absolutely essential area we must address because, as we have discussed, it is only together that we can navigate the huge tectonic shift that is about to take place. This has direct implications for how the market-based economy will evolve in the coming decades. Our capitalist system has fragmented, much like our communities have. Indeed, our capitalist system is one of our key communities. It must be repaired, and how we go about repairing it, preferably with a holistic solution, will make or break whether it survives.

BEYOND BOWLING ALONE

This fracturing of communities is something that has been explored for several decades now and it seems as though it is being exacerbated in today's world. In the year 2000, Robert Putnam published his seminal work *Bowling Alone: The Collapse and Revival of American Community* in which he achieved the tremendous feat of analysing historic data from the 1960s and comparing it to an equally tremendous survey across America in the late 1990s. He found that there was a drastic decline in what he called 'social capital'. Between the 1960s and 1990s, attendance at public meetings was down 35 per cent, serving on committees for local organizations was down 39 per cent, and membership rates for men's bowling leagues were down by 73 per cent.

At the turn of the millennium, it was clear that local communities had withered away. This trend is the same in Britain as well. Historian and writer Niall Ferguson found that the 2010 Citizenship Survey showed very similar findings, with only a quarter of people participating in any kind of formal voluntary work, and the share of people giving informal voluntary help to a local community at least once a month dropping from 35 per cent to 29 per cent.

Charitable giving has also fallen off a cliff in the UK. Beyond 'established' community works like charities, local governments and associations, the communities that used to act as a 'home' to individuals in a society have also been under assault. Family life has been in shambles, and the ongoing secularization of the West has meant that religious organizations, which used to be the centres of community and social cohesion, have had a smaller and smaller impact on people's lives with nothing meaningful developing to fill that space. Why has this happened? Well, for many commentators, the answers are fairly obvious: individualism.

Putnam, for example, blamed the rise of home TV and later the internet for this great degeneration of communities as people became more and more insular in their own lives and homes. And as we discussed in a previous chapter, Rabbi Jonathan Sacks has argued that a shift from 'We' to 'Me' in our public morality has caused this breakdown. Why would individuals commit themselves to a community and bind themselves to rules and regulations of that community when they can simply follow their own dreams? In turn, this has terrible implications for capitalism. The splitting up of communities indefinitely will be terminal for the market-based economy because the latter requires collaboration to work effectively. Even our financial structures reflect this need. They are designed to facilitate cooperation between shareholders, stakeholders and directors. Partnerships have, at the very foundation, the need for working together and distributing equitably to the participating partners; co-ventures reflect the desire for a joint venture between different financial or intellectual contributors, and co-investment shows a similar desire to draw in investments from very different constituent members.

Others take an 'economic individualistic' approach. For example, Paul Collier, author of *The Future of Capitalism*, argues that unchecked free markets were the cause of this breakdown. His view is that after the Second World War, there was an inherent sense of solidarity and community so that free markets were already 'regulated' by people's inherent moral commitments to each other, such that they sowed back into the community. But in the 1970s and 1980s, the great solidarity that comes from war subsided and a generation of individualistic profit-driven corporations began to bulldoze over community projects and initiatives. (What the impact of the shared-but-not-shared experiences of Covid will be in this respect will be interesting to see.) Technology further enabled this individualism by making the engines of inequality work even faster.

ZENNIALS AND NARCISSISM

Regardless, the analysis is generally the same. And it can be very easy to import this individualism to the Zennial generation. In fact, whole books have been written about it. Many people today say that Zennials are the most narcissistic, individualistic generation in the world. See Highsnobiety,[1] a global youth streetwear media brand, which posted a piece by Aleks Eror in 2020 entitled 'Social media has created a generation of self-obsessed narcissists'. He wrote:

> From deceptive selfie angles that make average looking people appear attractive, to curating your Facebook feed so it looks like you're having more fun than you actually are, social media has taken neoliberalism's self-centred mantra and pumped it full of cocaine-laced steroids. While Thatcher and Reagan may have promoted greedy self-interest that Renton lampooned in the original *Trainspotting*, social media has bloated humanity's capacity for self-obsession to new extremes … It has turned an entire generation into vapid narcissists.

In *The Narcissism Epidemic: Living in the Age of Entitlement*, psychologist Jean Twenge found that chart-topping pop songs were increasingly being filled with the word 'I' rather than 'We' between 1980 and 2007. Even *Vogue*, a magazine designed to celebrate the individuality of the fashion industry, published an article titled, 'Admit it, you love yourself: when did we become self-obsessed?'[2]

These quotes took me less than ten minutes to find – a simple search on Google for 'Self-Obsessed Generation' will garner about 16,600,000 results, most of which indict the Zennial (and anyone else with social media for that matter).

So, clearly, Zennials are just self-obsessed, attention-seeking narcissists addicted to Instagram likes, YouTube views and

Facebook comments, and set their hearts on getting on the 'For You Page' on TikTok. They are just continuing in the great tradition of 'individualism' that has defined the Western world for the last 200 years or so, and the breakdown of community and sense of belonging is just a continuation of what has been happening until now. They are the inhabitants of a terrifying Age of Delusion which will destroy the market economy. It feels like a closed case.

But herein lies the problem ... Zennials, as a whole, are not narcissistic individualists. Of course the media trope is that they are and there are obvious examples of such self-indulgence. The caricature of share, shag, shop is just that. Not least is it unacceptable to paint a whole generation in these broad strokes, but even if we were to do so in broad strokes, the result will not be coloured by narcissistic individualism. Spend a moment talking to someone between the ages of 18 to around 35, and you will quickly find that many of them are almost obsessively concerned about their community and society. In fact, coming across someone who was just 'out for number one' – which was the expectation when I started my job – would be the exception. The *me* to *we* shift is happening, though it is perhaps imperceptible to mainstream commentators. This is hugely important because it is 'we', not 'me', that will survive in the new capitalism.

Zennials have a hugely attuned sense of communitarian and collective action, a desire for a better world, a meaningful understanding of sacrifice for the greater good. On the point of narcissism, it strikes me that this generation is the one that lays the charge against themselves for their own narcissism. Surely, a narcissistic generation would not be concerned about how narcissistic they are. The common trait of a narcissist is that they are oblivious to how unpleasant their self-absorption is. Return to that *Vogue* article – 'When did we become so self-obsessed?' It is a self-indictment. It is what some religious people might call a conviction of sin; the recognition that something is deeply wrong with oneself even though overcoming it may be extremely difficult.

Tell Boomers that they are narcissists and they will castigate you for this accusation. Tell a Zennial that they are a narcissist and they may well agree with you! How un-narcissistic. Zennials have a desperate desire for belonging, connection, community and doing things together. The tide of individualism has shifted. But if this is the case, why have we not seen new communities arise from this generation to give them meaning and belonging? Why is it that this generation is often perceived as the loneliest generation? For example, one UK report from 2018 found that 40 per cent of respondents aged 16–24 reported feeling lonely often or very often, while only 29 per cent of people aged 65–74 and 27 per cent of people aged over 75 said the same.[3] That's surprising, and alarming. We normally consider the plight of lonely elders as a severe social problem (which it is!) but who would have thought that those between 16 and 24 were the ones who felt most isolated.

I think the answer to this lies in the ways in which Zennials are looking to come together, rather than in whether they are looking to come together. Zennials want to act together and collectively, but there is something preventing the 'collective' from becoming a 'community' – a group of people with a mutual bond of love and belonging.

Loved, known, noticed is a generational heartbeat. They want to belong and it's impressive to see how in hard times they reach out to each other. Many grew up with the TV series *Friends*, with its compelling theme of being a community looking out for each other. Zennials are a generation with joined-up writing linking the earth, justice and equality and their economic involvement. They want to see transformative acts. This is not simply finding a better way of making life easier but a deep commitment to a new discipleship. This is not simply life with a twist as if it were existing generational water with some new-gen flavouring. There is a deep-seated commitment to living in an integrated future. There is truth in the description of them as a caring, sharing and, yes, staring group.

THE SOVEREIGN INDIVIDUAL

Who controls you? Who is sovereign over you, your mind and your body?

Well, the answer is obvious isn't it? You, of course. Only *you* have the right to do what you like with your time, money, thoughts and actions. You are sovereign over your life and nobody else can make a meaningful claim to that. When it comes down to it, no government, no king or queen, no parent, no authority ought to be able to force you to do anything that you do not consent to. If they do, this is tyranny. An abuse of power.

This assumption is deeply embedded in us in the West. Regardless of generation, regardless of your political persuasions or commitments to your community, nothing is more real and certain than the individual – our sense of self. This is individualism. And it is perhaps one of the greatest achievements of the last 300 years. The individual is sovereign, and maximizing the liberty of the individual is of the most paramount importance. This is exemplified by John Stuart Mill in his 1859 book *On Liberty*: 'The only part of the conduct of any one, for which he is amenable to society, is that which concerns others. In the part which merely concerns himself, his independence is, of right, absolute. Over himself, over his own body and mind, the individual is sovereign.'

It's fairly in vogue nowadays to bash 'individualism'. We normally associate it with selfishness, egotism, a lack of compassion, and we blame many of the evils of our world on it. And unchecked neoliberalism. The planet is in ecological collapse because people only think about themselves, and so on.

However, the work of the individualists has reaped some of the most important and beautiful aspects of our modern world – from lofty things, such as formalizing the idea of inviolable rights for every individual, to the small wins of being able to break free from toxic traditions and expectations of your community that may perpetuate physical and moral violence in a culture. Without individualism, we'd lose the notion of having personal hopes and dreams. We'd lose the entrepreneurial and pioneering spirit that has come to define our times – which would perhaps represent the ultimate threat to capitalism.

We surely don't want to go back to a time when individuals are not empowered to pursue what is meaningful to them. Individualism is in many ways the mature fruit of a far more ancient tree: the theological concept of the *imago Dei*. The truth that every human creature is made in the image of the divine and worthy of infinite dignity and honour. It is a concept that is supremely aesthetic and beautiful to the eyes of those living in Western modernity. Indeed, nowhere better is it enshrined than in the US Declaration of Independence, in which 'certain unalienable Rights' are 'endowed to all men', among them 'Life, Liberty, and the Pursuit of Happiness'.

INDIVIDUALISM LOST

However, somewhere along the way, particularly during the years when Boomers came of age in the 1960s and 1970s, individualism became radicalized. Weaponized, even. A new fiat currency was formed: choice. Choice became the reserve currency of a generation.

For much of its history, individualism was still couched within a larger social context of religion and moral objectivity. The nations in which it flourished still had coherent moral structures and other 'sovereignties' against which individual freedom competed: God, Crown or Country. However, as these larger structures began to crumble, the individual became the only sovereign and, as New York pastor Tim Keller puts it, 'the freedom of the individual [became] a de facto absolute that vetoes all other things'.[4]

Individualist societies have not been able to balance individual freedom and broader communal obligations to family and community ever since and the consequences of this have been tragic for the Zennial generation. They have seen the dissolution of their parents' marriages in record numbers, and their societies grow increasingly fragmented with institutions breaking down and an unprecedented loss of social trust. Key social groups that maintain healthy human societies have crumbled because they necessarily require individuals to sacrifice some of their individual freedom to maintain them. Individualism became radical and wreaked havoc in the world. We lost sight of our interconnectedness, and the fact that there is no such thing as 'my' world.

THE CALL OF COLLECTIVISM

The Zennials have felt this pain. Many of them are pushing back against the radicalized individualism that has wreaked havoc on their personal lives, and feel that it is the cause of all the injustice they see in the world. And in doing so, they are being reintroduced to a serious contender to individualism: 'collectivism'. Under collectivism, 'collective human progress' is sovereign, not the individual. What really matters in the world isn't the atomized lives of individuals – instead, what matters is all of humanity coming together to pursue a single purpose with one heart and one mind. Individuals can only find true meaning with reference to the people around them and the purpose they serve together. Humans can rise above their small lives by being captured by a vision far greater than themselves. Climate change is a more important issue than any one of us, and our collective action in fighting it is of infinitely greater importance than any single life. Racial justice is a purpose we should all strive towards together, and it can only be achieved by means of collective action. It is a purpose that trumps our individual feelings.

This is collectivism and there is something very compelling about it. It appeals to something deeply noble in our humanity – it appeals to sacrifice, to vision, to a fight to be fought and a war to be won. It gives us the feeling of being caught up in something bigger than ourselves, looking to our right and to our left and seeing an army of people all facing in the same direction with one mind and purpose. This is beautiful stuff. This is what has captured the imagination of so many young people today. They feel a sense of togetherness where mutual self-giving births something more beautiful than the sum of its parts. Dare I say it, it feels like what I referred to earlier as CO. However, I believe that collectivism is a red herring. It promises so much, but it costs us too much and won't deliver the very thing that it promises: peace and purpose together.

It's always tempting for those who see the ugliness of radical individualism and the futility of an isolated self-absorbed existence to push for a revolution that strives for a goal that transcends our human experience and reality. This goal is almost always an abstract ideal that encourages individuals to give themselves to a greater cause, to sacrifice themselves on the altar of an unrealized future. I'm sure that many regimes and movements immediately spring to mind, as well as the evils they have wrought on our society throughout history. Collectivism played a key role in the regimes of both Joseph Stalin and Chairman Mao Zedong.

That should give us pause when it comes to viewing collectivism as a potential antidote to individualism.

It's true that moving away from radical individualism means that we learn to give ourselves away. 'How do we give ourselves away?' is the first question, but 'To whom do we give ourselves to?' is the second, and perhaps more urgent, question. Because we can indeed learn to give ourselves away and put our self-interest lower in our motivations, but there is a danger of giving ourselves to leaders, goals and movements that will ultimately cause further division and destruction, harnessing the crowd for whatever ends. True peace occurs when we give ourselves to each other, not to the ideals of various interest groups or individuals.

Collectivism is naturally utilitarian. It seeks the greatest good for the greatest number, and claims that the sum effort of a mass of individuals striving for a common goal is the means of achieving that good. What this fundamentally asserts, as Carl Jung pointed out in *The Undiscovered Self*, is that the individual simply becomes incidental and subordinate to the motivations of the abstract 'collective'. It imagines humanity as being a species that can somehow emerge into a 'higher consciousness' of the collective – much like some creature out of a science fiction tale or a hive of bees where the individual simply fulfils its role for the ongoing expansion of the hive.

The individual ceases to truly matter outside of the collective goal. However, you and I both know that humans are not such creatures. I, as an individual, experience a wholly unique and equally infinite reality just as you do – and no amount of empathy or emotional intelligence will be able to completely merge our subjective realities into a single experience. This is one of the most beautiful and terrifying aspects of being human. The sense that I cannot ever truly know another person and experience their life, but that a life lived well is a journey to truly know another person. The depth and measure of a human life cannot be compared or analysed – they are incommensurable. People matter individually, completely independent of other human individuals and without reference to a collective goal. This is the fundamental basis of human rights that we hold so dear – one of the greatest insights we have attained.

This is why the starvation of millions of Ukrainians under Soviet rule would be an unacceptable tragedy, even if the Soviet project was a resounding success and achieved global class equality for millennia to come. This is why the nuclear bombing of Hiroshima and Nagasaki will never have been 'good', even if it could be incontrovertibly proved that the two strikes prevented decades of bitter war that would have resulted in a far higher death count. However, utilitarians, and therefore collectivists, will say that so long as the ends are noble and achieved, the means are worth it no matter how devastating it might seem – we must look at the 'big picture' they will say. Don't get bogged down in the insignificant nuances of individual people or communities.

This is why collectivism cannot work. Not only is it an operating system for a different kind of species; it also undermines perhaps the most precious jewel of our civilization – the inviolable value of a human individual: the essence of our humanity. I belabour this point because the lure of collectivism always lurks in the background when it comes to CO – the solution of working together that I outlined earlier in this book. However, collectivism would destroy capitalism, CO will enhance it.

As the Zennial generation moves forwards and provides a corrective to the radical individualism of my generation, the siren song of collectivism will always play in the background ready to derail us. The Zennial generation has been disenchanted by the secular materialistic shallowness that my generation treasured so much. They are looking for another way, and in their disenchantment, the promise of becoming caught up in the battle for a transcendent visionary ideal is attractive.

But this means that this generation must itself always check that it does not slide into the pit of collectivism, in which lies the beasts of nationalism, extremism, polarization, elitism and expansionism. Much in the same way as my generation ought to have checked that we did not drift into the waters of radical individualism under which lie isolation, greed and the death of sacrifice and empathy.

RETURN TO COMMUNITY

The opposite of individualism, the antidote to it, and the ideal Zennials need to aim for is community, not collectivism. Collectivism is often held together by an adherence to some ideological commitment, and it is the ideology that matters most. The group identity of a community, on the other hand, emerges from the bonds between us – a web of relational ties that bind the group. Relational equity is the binding agent. The motivations of the community serve the individuals of the community together – there is no abstract 'community' that is beyond the individuals that make up the community.

These bonds are covalent. It is individuals offering themselves to each other in fraternity and love, sharing something of their lives with each other. It is a commitment to others and to civility. This shared life is what draws the group together and creates an authentic, and beautiful web of relationships that becomes a community. Communities can of course embark on great projects with lofty goals – and to great effect! However, their shared life will ensure the main thing stays the main thing – the flourishing of the human individuals that make up the community. When these come together at work, in a startup or venture capital company, a new force of market-based ingenuity is unleashed precisely because in community the individual contribution is not sacrificed to the collective ideal. Working in community is a powerful contribution to the way in which productivity and purpose become joined together.

Collectivism is bound by bonds of ideological allegiance. Community is bound by bonds of relational commitment. Collectivism is the enemy of true community.

There is a Zulu word that I used to hear when I was growing up in South Africa: '*Ubuntu*'. It loosely translates as 'I am because you are.' It is a somewhat nebulous and indistinct term to us. To an African it has a concrete and pervasive meaning, personal and commercial working together. It describes this conviction that our individual existence is not only enriched by other people, but existentially depends on other people. We cannot be saved alone, but only together. Zennials might not articulate it in those terms but I believe this is their heart-cry. Never lose sight of what is important in life – make the main thing the main thing. Abandon collectivism, and adopt community – a shared life, not simply a shared agenda. This is how communities are made. Doing life together in this way strengthens the common endeavour of creating economic value.

I believe that the vast majority of Zennials in fact desire this rather than collectivism. While minority extremist voices on every side dominate the press and media, I think most of the young people who will truly make a difference in our world are those passionate about people, and calling out for community. They desire more empathy, more collaboration, more compassion, and deeper connection with fellow humans rather than the coming of an abstract utopia. As we fight against the baseless emptiness of narcissism, let us not also trade our humanity to the churn of collectivism. Indeed, it is absolutely this that needs to be avoided for the future of capitalism to be a positive one.

5

THE END OF TRUTH

There is one final fissure we must address before moving on to the ways in which we solve the problems that face us in the Great Wealth Transfer, and that is the fissure of truth.

A couple of years ago, I found myself in Istanbul browsing in one of the famous Turkish bazaars. The energy is electric, the cacophony of shopkeepers and the clinks of lanterns keeps you alert and ready, you feel alive. Huge canvas bags of paprika, turmeric and other technicolour spices seduce the senses, and everywhere you turn, you see stalls selling gold, silver, bags, crockery, statues, vinyls, books – everything you can think of. As I was walking through this cauldron of human commerce, I saw a sign over a shop selling handbags that read: 'GENUINE FAKES – SOLD HERE'. I clearly remember asking myself the question: 'What is a *genuine fake*?' Drawn by this sign, I asked the shopkeeper my question: 'What do you mean, you sell genuine fakes? It can't be both …?'

The shopkeeper answered, 'No no no, you see, all the other handbags that are sold in this place are fake fakes. No one will sell you the genuine stuff. My cousin works at a Louis Vuitton factory on the other side of the city – when they produce handbags and belts, they have some that don't pass the quality test and are thrown out, so he brings them to me to sell here. So you see, these are genuine LV fakes!'

They were fake because LV would never actually sell them in a store due to their lack of quality, but they were also apparently genuine because they were slightly closer to the real thing than those sold by the other merchants out there. I thanked him and went on my way still thinking about this perplexing wording of 'genuine fake'. It raised a question in me about the genuineness of truth in our day. We live in a time when phrases like 'fake news' and 'alternative truth' are bandied around everywhere we turn. While my shopkeeper friend was dealing with genuine fake LV handbags and belts, I feel as though today, we are living in a world of genuine fake truths.

Truth is bought and sold, it is commoditized. We have entered a post-truth society. By this I mean that, whereas truth has always been assumed to be the bedrock of society, requiring no defence for its use but standing on its own and being intrinsically meaningful and objectively required for the working society and all the institutional and commercial structures within that society, this appears now not to be the case. The very nature of truth now has to be defended against those who would manipulate it for personal ends. 'My truth' and truth have become interchangeable. People accuse others of peddling fake truth while peddling a different kind of fake truth themselves. Some truths from some people are seen to be more genuine than others regardless of how factual they actually are.

It feels like we live in a wild west of Truth. We don't like talking about single sources of truth any more. You can get truth – or things that sound and feel like truth – from any back street of the internet today. Why go into a Louis Vuitton shop and pay the costly price for a genuine belt when you can get a genuine fake for 10 per cent of the price? Why pay the costly price of getting to the ultimate, genuine truth when you can get a genuine fake for 10 per cent of the effort? Least to say, there is a crisis of truth in our day and people are taking note. But it can also be an incredibly confusing and seemingly paradoxical matter to discuss in today's world.

Several years ago I remember advising a luxury goods company and asking the owner about fake watches. He had a simple view that they were not a threat to business because people did not want to live with a wristwatch knowing it was a fake, as it made them feel demeaned and cheap. I wonder whether this would still apply today?

WHAT IS TRUTH?

I remember in the 1990s, people were talking about post-modernism and how our society had become 'relativist', particularly around morality. This idea that there is no such thing as objective 'good' and 'bad' and that everyone could just hold whatever opinions they wanted so long as we left each other alone. Just don't hurt anyone, try to be a good person in the way you see fit, and get on with life.

I also remember back then that people were arguing that we had succumbed to 'scientism' – not to be confused with 'scientist'. The idea that the 'truth' can only be attained through science and mathematics. Richard Dawkins was quite a prominent figure in the early years of the twenty-first century. He and other prominent scientists like Stephen Hawking promoted this view, particularly looking to discount all 'spiritual knowledge' as saying anything meaningfully 'true'.

These two views – relativism and scientism – are quite consistent with each other, and are fairly easy to understand. Truth can be found through evidence-based empirical analysis. This is the most reliable way to get at the truth.

This view is, of course, very limiting and discounts the vast swathes of human experience and knowledge, but I appreciate its consistency.

Today, this is not the case. When Boomers now interact with Zennials, we come up against an opaque barrier of understanding. We throw around words like 'post-truth' in the press, and we presume it means 'relativist' in the way we used to talk in the 1990s.

But then we turn around and we encounter huge crowds of Zennials having very deep convictions about what is right, good and true, and asserting it as gospel truth. (Would we still use this phrase today to describe the gold standard by which truth is measured?) That doesn't sound very relativist. Not only that, even the laid-back approach of 'you-do-you' and 'that's your opinion' no longer seems to work any more. It's often the case now that if you are of a certain group of people, your opinions and point of view are tainted and less legitimate based on the colour of your skin or your gender, or your age, while if you are of a different group, your perspective is gilded with special truth-telling power. At the same time, Zennials are far more open to liminal ideas, and different ways of looking at the world. They are embracing spirituality and less scientific ways of thinking. It seems as though they are at once less relativist and less certain about how to get to that truth yet seemingly more certain about what truth is.

The war in Ukraine has made a major contribution to killing off the notion that truth is only in the eye of the beholder. Vladimir Putin has made it clear that his truth is the legitimate annexation of Ukraine. No longer can this defence hold when faced with the onslaught of evil which has rightly been attacked as such in clear, compelling and objective terms.

Ask a Zennial if they think that truth can only be deduced scientifically, and they would raise an eyebrow. Felt experience, marginal stories and liminal spaces are of great worth to them. Even within the sciences, Svend Brinkmann astutely observes that the custodians of truth of our day have moved from the hard scientists like Hawking or Dawkins, to the social scientists like sociologist Jonathan Haidt or psychologist Jordan Peterson. It used to be the mysteries of the universe that drove our search for truth. Today, it seems to be the mysteries of the human heart and communities. And science is found wanting at unravelling those mysteries. Like it or not, these mysteries will feature in the workplace and will need to be addressed by every corporation seeking a fulfilled cohort of Zennial employees.

THE EPISTEMOLOGICAL CRISIS

I have personally found it confusing engaging in many of the contemporary debates with the young people around me because the way we approach 'truth' has so fundamentally changed. These are questions of epistemology: how we know what we know, and what measure we use to determine the truth. That our literature on the topic is so complex and crowded points to the fact that there is a new epistemological pluralism, or an epistemological crisis hovering over our world. We're not entirely sure how to get at the truth any more. We're not quite sure where it comes from. We don't quite know how to recognize genuine fakes from fake fakes or genuine genuines.

Over the last 50 years, it has been a valid concern that we have limited what it means for something to be 'true'. As I said before, it was the case that science had the exclusive claim to determine and interpret reality. But for Zennials, the walls that have been built around the ultimate truth of science are crumbling. Clearly there are truths that are unattainable through those means. The truth of love cannot simply be reduced to biology; the truth about someone's mental health cannot be reduced to psychological theories. Someone who can empathize with the other can be said to have ascertained a 'truth' that someone who simply studies emotions has not. To understand someone is different to knowing about someone. There are real truths that can't simply be measured. And we should call them truths, not simply opinions, emotions and experiences. Broadening our epistemological horizons is a good thing, and it is something that Zennials have championed. It seems particularly true that subjective, experiential realities are of great importance to Zennials, that there is something true about the world to be found in understanding the experiences of specific individuals.

Zennials are also far more pluralistic in their approach to truth. Boundaries and limits are not good currency for the Zennials. Latitude, flexibility, openness and fluidity are all philosophical concepts more honed by this generation than previous ones. Zennials are flexitarian in their philosophical outlook and any interaction with them that does not take this way of thinking and action into account will flounder. Herein lies the challenge. While Boomers may well be accused of rigidity and dogmatic attitudes, these divides need to be bridged and learnings must be taken from both. There are great benefits to seeking stability and wanting to derive a singular truth, just as there are benefits to plurality and prioritizing the seeking over the stability.

This is a potentially positive route to go down – we can come to a richer, more full understanding of TRUTH that incorporates both the insights and experiences of multiple disciplines, experiences and generations. Perhaps we will once again see a pursuit of 'truth' in disciplines like morality and religion that do not depend on scientific observation. However, today, the benefits of a pluralistic epistemology are not being felt.

Instead, this pluralism has been a force for greater fracturing rather than healing. We dissolved the monopoly that science had on truth, opening up new ways of understanding the world for fresh expression and legitimacy. But instead of a richer understanding of truth, we have fractured it into a million pieces and we continue to step on the shards to make it even more impossible to get at the truth of the matter. And one of the primary reasons for this is the Zennial adoption of what is known as critical theory.

NO SUCH THING AS TRUTH

The last 50 years has seen the accelerated rise of these disciplines, a fruit (but perhaps not the intentions) of French postmodernist thinkers like Jean-François Lyotard, Michel Foucault and Jacques Derrida. It is a way of seeing the world, knowledge and truth claims purely and singularly in terms of the application of power.

The world is primarily seen through the lens of power differentials. Culture itself is a deeply layered web of oppression, and any structure that exists, be it institutional, corporate, linguistic or epistemological, reinforces this oppression. Foucault argued that the ways in which we determine truth, scientific or otherwise, are simply culturally devised systems that define what can be seen as legitimate or illegitimate rather than systems that help us pursue the real truth. As soon as you put parameters around knowledge, you invoke oppression because you give power to the people who are playing the right 'epistemological game'.

These structures are then perpetuated by the way society talks about things – by 'discourses' – which legitimizes this way of seeing truth. In this world, any form of categorization and boundaries is viewed with deep suspicion. Any process by which we can get at the truth needs to be held at arm's length. The process itself is an application of abusive power.

There have been many thoughtful people throughout history who have advocated against black-and-white binary thinking. Whether it is the Eastern vision of Yin and Yang in which both sides of the binary are co-dependent, or the Christian understanding of a complex being who is both fully God and fully man, we have always felt that the truth would transcend sharp categorizations and yes/no answers. We have always known that the line between black and white is not a sharp divide but infinite shades of grey. However, this is not the approach of the postmodernists.

For them, there are no shades, everything is grey, and the labels black or white are purely cultural constructs to keep certain people out. Traditional non-binary ways of seeing the world were always driven by a desire to truly get at the full picture of the truth, to see in higher resolution. Critical theory is driven by the scepticism that we simply cannot know the truth, and that the search for it is not only futile, but dangerous. Foucault went as far as to say that we live in 'regimes of truth' that entrap us.

The intellectual influence of these French postmodernists is far-reaching and broad. According to the Google Scholar database, Foucault has become the most influential academic in a generation, having been cited in over one million academic papers. It is no understatement that many university subject courses owe their existence to his ideas and the ideas of his peers, be it Gender Studies, Queer Theory or Critical Race Theory. Neither would it be an understatement to say that many of the core ideas that shape conversations around justice and ethics today, such as Kimberlé Crenshaw's 'Intersectionality', are built on their shoulders. This way of seeing the world says that there is no such thing as truth – none at all. Not even scientific truth is reliable. Knowledge, which in common language means 'an accurate understanding of objective reality', is simply an illusion and the very ways in which we decide what is true are based on categories that are culturally enforced.

The rabbit hole of critical theory goes deep but academic Helen Pluckrose helpfully lays out some important core ideas that underpin this worldview:

- There are no ways of attaining objective truth; everything is culturally constructed.
- Society is dominated by different systems of power.
- The categories we use to differentiate fact and fiction, emotion and reason, science and art, male and female are false. They are all in the service of power. These categories need to be broken down.
- Language is not amoral; it is used to construct oppressive social realities and must be regarded with suspicion.
- The idea of the autonomous individual is a myth.
- There is no such thing as a universal human nature.

She goes on to write:

[In this new critical posture] shared humanity and individuality are essentially illusions and people are propagators or victims of discourses depending on their social position; a position which is dependent on identity far more than their individual engagement with society.

Morality is culturally relative, as is reality itself. Empirical evidence is suspect and so are any culturally dominant ideas including science, reason, and universal liberalism. These are Enlightenment values which are naïve, totalizing and oppressive, and there is a moral necessity to smash them. Far more important is the lived experience, narratives and beliefs of "marginalized" groups all of which are equally "true" but must now be privileged over Enlightenment values to reverse an oppressive, unjust and entirely arbitrary social construction of reality, morality and knowledge.

The only truth in a world like this is the existence of oppressive and cultural constructs. This is the only objective reality. The true nature of the world and human society is only adversarial, violent and different groups trying to dominate each other. The only way forward is to continually expose and destroy these oppressive cultural constructs over and over again. In short, many of those who adhere to critical theory are 'seek[ing] to reject the entire scientific enterprise in favour of a knowledge that flows from identity ... tradition, folklore, interpretation and emotion'.[1]

THE END OF DEBATE

These ideas used to only exist in a dark corner of the academic world, but they have entered the mainstream and underpin much of the Zennial conversation today. They are at the heart of much of the conflict we experience politically, generationally and personally. And the economy is no exception. They have become central to global issues like race, sexuality, nations, borders, and what it means to be human and live together. And, of course, as a result they have an everyday impact on our economies and corporations.

Postmodern critical theory is perhaps the greatest barrier facing intergenerational collaboration and conversation because it delegitimizes certain people purely on the basis of what group identities they are a part of. This naturally pits people against each other and always looks to divide and conquer, rather than come together and collaborate. The cancel culture is at the centre of this generational shift, with serious consequences in the way in which a new orthodoxy is taking hold of the culture that demonizes those holding contrary views to the prevailing consensus. Freedom of speech, the bedrock of democracy and quintessentially the foundation of the market economy, is under existential threat.

Questioning is seen as dissidence, institutions are seen as one-dimensional proliferators of oppression, and even the idea of debate, a fundamental ingredient to establishing truth together, is viewed with suspicion.

In an article for the *Independent* published in July 2020, Nadia Whittome, a UK Labour MP, wrote:

> We must not fetishize "debate" as though debate is itself an innocuous, neutral act. If someone wanted to initiate a debate about whether women are innately less intelligent than men or whether disabled people should be paid the same level of wages as non-disabled people, we would rightly be appalled at such a suggestion. The very act of debate in these cases is an effective rollback of assumed equality and a foot in the door for doubt and hatred.

Whittome is a Zennial. Indeed, she is the current 'Baby' of the House of Commons – the youngest MP – having been born in 1996.

Universities, which have always been bastions for developing academic freedom and the pursuit of truth, have wobbled under these postmodern Zennial pressures of no-platforming, cancelling, and denying free speech for fear that invisible and all-pervasive structures of oppression will be reinforced simply by the act of considering alternative, competing positions. A recent study from the Heterodox Academy, a research body dedicated to preserving academic freedoms, found that 55 per cent of student respondents in the US agreed that the climate on their campus prevents students from saying things they believe.

Further research has shown that academics and professors themselves are feeling the chilling effect of these postmodern pressures. In a survey, 445 academics in US universities were asked: 'Imagine expressing your views about a controversial issue while at work, at a time when faculty, staff, and/or other colleagues were present. To what extent would you worry about the following consequences?' To the hypothetical 'My reputation would be tarnished', 32.68 per cent answered 'very concerned' and 27.27 per cent answered 'extremely concerned'. To the hypothetical 'My career would be hurt', 24.75 per cent answered 'very concerned' and 28.68 per cent answered 'extremely concerned'. Essentially, over half of the academics surveyed felt growing pressure from forces of illiberalism and intellectual tribalism to not express themselves.

It is in these environments that a generation that is now joining the workforce has been moulded. This will have profound effects on how decisions are made and corporate strategy determined and implemented in the future.

Not all Zennials subscribe to all the conclusions of the postmodernists. In fact, I doubt most of them do. Most young people deeply value constructive, lively debate; are willing to think deeply about competing evidence and come to non-partisan conclusions; and seek nothing more than reconciliation and harmony with their ideological opponents.

Indeed, it was heartening to see recently that a debate at the Cambridge Union overwhelmingly voted in favour of the motion: 'This house believes in the right to offend'.[2]

However, the postmodern approach has become the water we are swimming in today, and it is important that we recognize the intellectual heritage this worldview is rooted in and the conclusions it comes to. Much of the rhetoric has the ability to tap into the collaborative, compassionate and connected heart of Zennials, but it utilizes their goodwill and energy in service of a worldview that is deeply pessimistic and toxic. It removes any possibility of intergenerational – or even intra-generational – collaboration and creation of something new and beautiful. It does not allow for a vision to be set for a future because of its scepticism towards any grand narrative. It hijacks the compassion and activist heart of the Zennial generation to pursue purely destructive ends.

In this way, the objective nature of truth has become undermined. And it has become even more exacerbated in the era of fake news, which has taken on a life of its own and its own justification. Disinformation and the breakdown of trust in the media reinforces this worldview: that we really can't trust anybody who claims to have something true to say. We can only pick and choose which source feels most correct and adopt the principle that truth lies in the mind of the speaker. 'My truth' becoming equivalent to 'the truth'.

Covid exaggerated this clash of objectivity and subjectivity onto the global stage. In a realm as certain and objective as medical science, truth should have been something that was easier to agree upon. But this was not the case. From all sides, truth became increasingly determined by what people subjectively wanted to believe. Sometimes, 'The Science' was used as a measure of absolute objective truth and governments

121

or the press used it as a test of absolute certainty. The reality, of course, is that the development of scientific knowledge around Covid was an ever-changing, adapting body of work that shifted every day as new evidence came to light. Just as it should have done.

However, people trusted it as if it were the only truth that could possibly save us. I'm not meaning to say that we should not have trusted the science, but every scientist will tell you that during the 2020 pandemic, the real truth about the virus was constantly changing because they were constantly learning new things about it. The press and the public, however, simply clung on to whichever statistic or scientific statement seemed to fit what they wanted to be true and presented it as objective fact. Scientific knowledge became used to affirm a subjective hunch.

At other times, it was outrageous conspiracy theories that became elevated as having the status of truth, from rumours about 5G telecoms towers causing the virus to misinformation about cures you could effect at home. These conspiracies were the objective truths discovered by certain individuals that affirmed their subjective biases. During a time of intense anxiety, and fear, we simply did not know what truth was any more. This has revealed that we have become woefully untrained at establishing truth. This has deep consequences for capitalism.

WHY TRUTH MATTERS

Trust in the sources of truth is a very important factor. In Deloitte's 2019 Global Millennial Survey – which was based on the views of 13,416 Millennials across 42 countries, as well as 3,009 Gen Zers from ten countries – around 45 per cent, so nearly half, said they have 'absolutely no trust' in either political or religious leaders as sources of reliable and accurate information, and 27 per cent have zero trust in the media as a source of reliable and accurate information.[3] More recently, the 2022 Edelman Trust Barometer (which is not generationally specific) came up with similar findings, with nearly one out of two respondents viewing government (48 per cent) and media (46 per cent) as divisive forces in society.[4]

These are staggering figures and are symptomatic of a serious breakdown of trust. One thing we must commit to going forwards is to rebuild trust between institutions and individuals. Trust is built one deal at a time over decades, but it can be knocked down in a single moment and we are living in the aftermath of one such collapse. Indeed, the single most important reason for the collapse of the financial system in the Global Financial Crisis was the breakdown in trust.

Alongside this, the information age has made it more possible than ever before to spread what is untrustworthy. For all their helpfulness, algorithms have shown their power to govern almost every aspect of our digital lives and minds. Artificial intelligence and search algorithms have become dominant forces in determining how we know what we know in our day – the information age has become somewhat of an algocracy. Algorithms are no longer simply a tool for dealing with vast data sets, they are now a code that can harness, for better or for worse, our emotional, financial or private interests, and that can project us into categories that we had no choice about joining.

Digital platforms like YouTube, Instagram and TikTok rely almost entirely on advertising revenue to keep their companies afloat. These are companies that sell human attention and so it is very much in their interest that users stay on their platforms. Search algorithms play a central role in making this happen by serving users content that the algorithm thinks they will like, getting better at it over time as more information is collected. This, in and of itself, is not a bad thing. Tailored digital content is hugely beneficial in a landscape that has more information than any one person can handle. Search algorithms are simply mirrors that reflect and magnify where your true interests lie. You may claim that you are a jazz enthusiast but your Spotify recommendations will be the true test of that fact. The issue lies where it is reflecting and magnifying an aspect of our humanity that ought not be magnified: fear, paranoia, and the temptation to form tribal lines.

Algorithms can become well programmed, simply by using them, to exploit the anxiety loops within our day-to-day living. Catastrophizing and considering the worst outcomes in any given situation grow as stress levels increase and we retreat into a claustrophobic emotional world. So truth claims give way to those that would exploit human weakness. It is no wonder that Zennials have turned inwards, and trust only what they can experience first hand – what is subjective.

The breakdown of trust in the authorities of truth, and the corrosive worldview of the postmodern critical theorists, has resulted in a kind of epistemological and moral panic that has hit the Zennial generation. It has tried to evaluate a code of living well together while failing to articulate any objective tests for these moral judgements. There is a recognition that there cannot just be an 'anything goes' moral test, but they are yet unwilling to stake their flag in the ground to establish some moral foundation.

This has sometimes resulted in an extraordinary feature wherein Zennials can deal with moral inconsistencies in an unfazed manner, holding quite often two opposing moral views at exactly the same time without feeling any discomfort. For example, climate change is the biggest danger to our society, yet a lifestyle of travel and flight is an aspirational lifestyle. Or take crypto and the huge environmental damage done through mining Bitcoin which has not deterred the Zennial passion for the tokens. What I recognize in this curious mixture is the morality of the 'WE' with the motivation of the 'I'. The 'we' dominates aspirationally as a kind of ethical imperative for living well for the common good. However, the motivation of the first-person-singular 'I' still lurks in the background as narcissism and it is the big ethical vampire squid entangling a generation. In other words, Zennials want to be a generation that puts the WE first – but feel trapped by internal desires and temptations to still look out for number one – 'I'. A multi-faceted, pluralist approach to truth and morality has its benefits, but it makes it difficult to identify these kinds of inconsistencies.

I find it remarkable that Professor Michael Sandel of Harvard has the best-attended classes in the university. His lectures on ethics and justice command the full attention of a generation struggling to determine true moral behaviour. The content of his curriculum is not outrageously unique – he offers the foundational building blocks of moral reasoning and political science. However, the way he runs his lectures is notable.

He gets students to debate with each other on moral reasoning and questions of justice ranging from simple ethics questions all the way to complex political theories, acting as a mediator, moderator and clarifier of the debate. He is a curator of the debate and, in some ways, a curator of truth. Despite the dominance of critical theorists in university campuses and in the activist movements around the world, there is a deep hunger in the Zennial generation to discover what is true, and to do it together – Professor Sandel seems to recognize this and sees the potential of contemporary technology to facilitate this on a scale never before seen.

In a Ted talk he said: 'Wouldn't it be interesting to take this way of thinking and arguing, engaging seriously with big moral questions, exploring cultural differences, and connect a live video hookup with students in Beijing, and Mumbai, and in Cambridge, Massachusetts and create a global classroom – that's what I'd love to do.'

EXPOSING WIKIMORALITY

Wikimorality cannot be the way forwards: the kind that is peer-reviewed and established through popular vote rather than a meaningful authority – the kind of moral reasoning where we can cut, paste and edit different truth and moral claims to create a nonsensical collage. It cannot guide us in a consistent and meaningful way. It may seem like inclusivity, but it is in reality the erasure of true beautiful diversity. Compromise, persuasion and conversation between different moral standpoints is the aim, not the flattening out of the moral landscape of humanity – humanity is not beige; it is an explosion of technicolour. Pope Francis writes:

> I cannot truly encounter another unless I stand on firm foundations, for it is on the basis of these that I can accept the gift the other brings and in turn offer an authentic gift of my own. I can welcome others who are different, and value the unique contribution they have to make, only if I am firmly rooted in my own people and culture.

This is timeless wisdom: true inclusivity does not mean being uncommitted and unable to make up our minds; it means being committed to a foundation but willing to change our minds. We need to be people who recognize that irreconcilable differences do not necessarily lead to charged conflict and that living well together does not mean ideological purity.

The discovery of truth, like all meaningful human endeavours, is a strenuous, difficult and long process. It cannot be won through a Google search or a conversation on Twitter but it requires patience and commitment. This is the path to wisdom.

And on this journey, we must start with our feet on solid ground. We will never discover the truth if our primary posture is to never commit to anything until it is 100 per cent accurate and seek to deconstruct every inaccuracy to its component parts – we cannot afford to always 'start anew'.

Truth will flow when there is a humble exchange of ideas between people who are committed to their ideals, but humble enough to receive as a gift the differences of the other. Young people today desire universality and openness – but this committed approach prevents us from a 'false openness' that is 'born of the shallowness of those lacking insight into the genius of their native land or harbouring unresolved resentment towards their own people'.

I encourage young people not to spurn their historic culture and those who have come before them. Not because they are the most virtuous, or the most wise, but because having a foundation is better than having none. It is always better to move forwards unburdened by self-hatred and resentment. Moral sobriety and consistency is desperately needed today – we cannot be reactionary when it comes to truth.

A RETURN TO TRUTH

In the coming decades there will be a greater realization that truth matters, as truth is an essential building block for a functioning and flourishing civil society and underwrites the drivers of the market economy aimed at preserving our liberties. In this debate the Boomer contribution is of real significance. This is perhaps the fight for the soul of a generation.

The English poet John Milton asked in his *Areopagitica*, one of history's most influential and impassioned philosophical defences of the principle of a right to freedom of speech and expression: 'Let her [Truth] and Falsehood grapple; who ever knew Truth put to the worse in a free and open encounter?'

But he was reckoning without the emotional responses, the prejudices of cultures, vested interests and social media, that can sway the ethical perceptions of a generation. This is why we have a truth crisis on our hands.

Zennials may be sceptical but they're not gullible. It can be easy for Boomers to simply throw the charge that young people don't care about truth and objective facts, that they are just led by emotions and the whims of their so-called hearts. But from what I've observed, Zennials are desperately thirsty for truth and want to seek it out truly. I think one reason why postmodern critical theory is so appealing to young people is that it offers an account and interpretation of human truths rather than an individualistic scientific approach to society. It appeals to the relational and communitarian impulses of the Zennial, in the same way that collectivism does. And as I have said already, Zennials care, and they care deeply, and for people to care they need to stand on a truth that they can believe in.

Fortunately, I don't see a long future for postmodern critical theory. I am not alone. Simon Jenkins, in his review of Pluckrose and James Lindsay's book *Cynical Theories* in the *Times Literary Supplement*, wrote: 'I am sure this moment will pass, but I sense we are glimpsing one of those side-tracks in Western ideology that led to both Salem and Weimar.'[5]

I was a student leader in South Africa during the Apartheid years and chaired the academic freedom committee in my university in Johannesburg. We committed ourselves to fighting for a university in which any person, regardless of race, colour, creed or gender could join in the pursuit of knowledge. All universities at the time were segregated and only whites were allowed to attend my university. In looking back I am grateful for the efforts that we made to keep alive the belief that freedom of speech was the foundation of democracy and the guarantee of liberty. All of which were denied by the then government. Since then I have retained an unwavering passion to defend freedom of speech and the pursuit of truth particularly in our universities where the danger signals are already flashing. It is incomprehensible to me that a new generation might grow up in these citadels of learning dedicated to the expression of views even when inimical to others and try to prevent the free and fair expression of thought.

Anyone on the side of truth and who is passionate about building up will always push back against this deconstructive mode. The true unfettered exchange of ideas will reign supreme for communities who value truth, and free speech will be protected when these communities reflect on the world. It simply takes one high-profile institution to push back against the demands of critical theory to explode the myth that the loud minority voices are in fact the majority. Indeed, even in the height of the culture wars among students, Cambridge University made a strong decision to protect Freedom of Expression, saying that 'It's our duty to tolerate colleagues even when they say things that we consider foolish, when we find their views offensive we should point that out politely. We should not be running to the vice chancellor asking him to censor them.'

Mob mentality comes and goes in flashes and I believe that the silent majority of Zennials will uphold and embrace the free exchange of ideas in civil debate and move past this culture war. Only then can we quench our thirst for truth.

One Zennial working in the advertising industry insightfully writes:

> Despite the rhetoric and soundbites of 'You-do-you' and 'live your own truth', our content consumption betrays that we do not in fact live like this. Most urban cores of globalised cities are not full of dire existentialists and complete moral relativists. Rather, they are filled with individuals and communities deeply passionate about their health and wellbeing, ambitious about living a fulfilling rich life, and even engaged with the grave injustices and terrors of modern life – if apathy is found, it's generally from the fear of feeling overwhelmed with care rather than lacking it altogether.

Least to say we don't, in fact, live in a post-truth world. If we did, we wouldn't have adverts like the recent campaign from the *New York Times* which simply read: Truth. It's more important now than ever.

For an advertising agency to be able to convince one of the highest-profile publications in the world to buy such an audacious, inflammatory ad campaign requires them to be absolutely certain (or at least present it that way) that it will work. Months of data analysis, sociological study, ethnographic profiling and market research will have had to be done to convince the *New York Times* that what people genuinely care about today is TRUTH.

But we cannot just take the path back to truth for granted. We must build it together. We must rediscover the importance of truth – and have the conviction to be able to commit to the objectivity of truth: that there is indeed a singular truth, no matter how complex, that we are moving towards together. The Zennial generation has a remarkable open-mindedness, but as G. K. Chesterton writes: 'Merely having an open mind is nothing. The object of opening the mind, as of opening the mouth, is to shut it again on something solid.'

The market economy cannot exist without the clear buy-in of all participants in the market. Every prospectus of a new share being brought to the public market goes through a laborious verification process to determine the veracity of every statement that is contained in this document. It is important because it's on the basis of what is disclosed that investors make their investment decisions. Similarly research into companies relies upon executives giving accurate and truthful answers to questions. Again this is the very essence of the way in which a market economy works. If truth is under threat then the market economy will simply not function.

This, then, is the challenge that faces us ahead of the Great Wealth Transfer. We have the benefactors and the beneficiaries at each other's throats and unable to agree on anything, much less a way to advance together. We have a capitalism unfit for the challenges of the twenty-first century and unacceptable to those who need to be its advocates if it is to survive. We have advancing technology that could be the tool that unites and brings us together in harmony, but that instead divides us in ways we didn't think possible. We have communities broken by individualism that are struggling to heal and, as a result, are leading many Zennials potentially towards the lure of collectivism. And we have a world in which it is difficult, perhaps near impossible, to establish objective truth.

These are the threats that, if not dealt with, will lead to the end of capitalism and society as we know it. These threats are present the world over and are existential. They will not be combated by conflict. If we carry on down the antagonistic path we are on, we will not find unity and togetherness at the end; we will find fissures and bitterness and an unfixable system.

But we are not there yet.

6

UNDERSTANDING CO

I said at the opening of this book that there is a narrow path that leads us to a more inclusive, purposeful and reformed capitalism rather than a way that wreaks havoc on our society. The foundation of this is what I have named CO. This shift from *me* to *we*. At its core, CO's essentials are the shift away from individualism towards collaboration, compassion, community and collective experience, and the understanding that we give up far less than we gain by acting together. Crucially, it is also the understanding, so essential to the survival of capitalism, that Zennials and Boomers need to work together for the best outcome, because it is only the blend of insight and hindsight that will see us take the narrow path we need to.

I will explore and explain CO much further in the remainder of this book – CO-leading, CO-working, CO-compassion, CO-creating, CO-destiny – providing a toolkit for how we avoid catastrophe and engender reconciliation.

THE DUNNING–KRUGER EFFECT

Have you ever been inspired to take up a new craft? Perhaps you once saw chess grandmasters engaged in a battle of wits and strategy and were so compelled by the exchange that you wanted to pick up the game for the first time in your life. Or maybe you walked past a busker on the street playing the main theme from *Schindler's List* on the violin and just had a moment of epiphany that nothing would make you happier than to be the type of person who could produce that kind of beauty with your hands and a piece of wood. For most people, such an epiphany is a passing fantasy or an aspiration, a bit like the thought of winning the Lottery. You enjoy the mental exercise of thinking to yourself how nice it would be to be a grandmaster or a violin savant, and then move on with your life. Sometimes, though, we can move beyond that fantasy and actually commit to taking the first steps, putting some investment into buying that chess set or beginner's violin (the latter being quite a significant investment, in fact). And more often than not, one of two things happens.

With something like chess, what you might find is that you can memorize how each piece moves, learn a couple of standard openings, and off you go. You play your first games and, particularly if you are taking it up with your equally amateur peers, your confidence as a budding chess grandmaster explodes through the roof even though your adventure into the craft has been incredibly short-lived and you probably couldn't hold a candle to the primary-school chess champion. This is something that's called the Dunning–Kruger effect, when your confidence and true abilities are at odds.

When you plot a graph of 'Confidence' against 'Experience', you see a huge spike at the start where confidence in one's abilities is completely disproportionate to competence. However, what you then see is that as someone gains experience in a field, as they become more and more competent, their confidence declines significantly to the point that, even when they are really quite good at what they do, they are racked with insecurity and lack of self-belief.

I've seen this in many students who attend top-class universities and who I have worked alongside. On almost any objective scale they are incredibly intelligent, articulate and competent. However, they walk around overflowing with self-doubt while people in far less academically rigorous universities are filled with self-assurance. Only after somebody becomes a true expert does their confidence align appropriately to their competence.

If the chess-playing Dunning–Kruger effect is one extreme, the other is what can happen when you take up something like the violin. And if you've ever had the misfortune of sharing a home with children practising the violin you will know that there are few things as antithetical to beauty than the noise that comes out of the instrument held by those beautiful, yet accursed, hands.

We all understand that learning a new craft is hard work. But we often forget how ungratifying the first hundred or thousand steps can really be. The main theme from *Schindler's List* is beautiful. But in order to gain the skills to play such a piece, it first requires years and years of practising banal scales and arpeggios. However, there are those people who would pick up the violin and try to go straight into playing the beautiful pieces. They will slavishly sink weeks into one bar at a time, never learning to master the instrument but bent on producing one piece. The learning curve for something like the violin is particularly steep and requires years of sounding like two foxes in the night before you can get to anything resembling art. More often than not, people who choose to take up an instrument in their adult years will abandon it fairly quickly due to the amount of devotion, time and grit required to get good at it.

But why am I talking about this? What has it to do with CO or how we succeed in working together? Well, it's because CO is fundamentally not too dissimilar to a craft to be mastered rather than a theory to be taught – we all learn our crafts from others. This is one of its key attractions, because we can all learn it. It is a craft that has captured our imaginations even if we don't give it the name CO.

THE CO ROUTE

CO strikes at the heart of our generation's greatest aspirations. We have awakened to the desire for an integrated, holistic vision of human living, casting off the radical individualism and shallowness that has defined our society for so long. We are desperate for true connection and are longing for simple ways to enact change together in our complex times. Today, we seek community and connection from the smallest scale of friend relationships to the grandest of the multilateral governance of the world. However, despite this longing, we are also susceptible to not hitting the mark and end up being tragically ill-equipped to bring about healing.

In this, we also experience all the challenges of trying to master a craft. There are some who fall foul of the Dunning–Kruger effect, who will proclaim themselves as having the super-drug cure to all of our society's ailments, exhibiting all the confidence in the world despite being only a few years into their activism or research. There are claims that this single fix, this super app, this undiscovered political system, this leader, will be the thing that will transform the world. This is not the route.

Then there are those other fresh-faced dreamers who have lofty CO ambitions. Perhaps their dream is to establish a global creative community to rejuvenate the arts in the Western world but they lack the years of grind and graft to make it a reality. The Zennial generation is filled with idealism and this is a wonderful thing. However, making CO a reality will require more than idealism. It will require years of practice and test-and-learning. It will require us to harmonize many of the human impulses that are at work within us as a community. This is the harder route. But the one that will succeed.

We have to take into account the true nature of people, the pace of change and the current state of the world – as explained in previous chapters – to press on forwards without leaving too many behind. We need to recognize that institutional capitalists exist who want to do good, or that people have deep spiritual attachments and commitments, or that a nation's culture means something to people. We cannot afford to be tunnel-visioned and turn our noses up at industries and communities that seem to hold intuitions that are different from our own. We must ask the question, 'Who can I partner with?' rather than 'Who can I fight against?' This is absolutely fundamental to achieving CO. Because that latter question seems to be the one that many jump to ask these days. We are constantly putting ourselves at odds with something else that we don't like. This is how we end up in our silos. Our echo chambers. This has to end if we are to work effectively together. We must always seek to inhabit the intersection. Otherwise, we risk becoming revolutionaries, not reformers. And revolutions almost always end in oceans of blood.

I speak about this partly from my own experience of life. As I have mentioned, I have spent the best part of my entire professional career in the most established of establishments: the banks and financial institutions in the

City of London. Having been in the middle of the storm during the 2008 Global Financial Crisis and having lived through countless booms and busts – including the current crisis in the banking system – I am incredibly cognizant of the amount of power that the financial institutions carry in the world.

It is no wonder that Zennials have gone after them with great force. From the outside, they seem to be the new autocrats of our global economy. Things seem to happen behind closed doors in huge glass towers with a few old men apparently playing games with hundreds of billions of dollars.

Of course, there is greed and mismanagement in these institutions, but things are not that simple and I believe there are principles from that world that are crucial for a more united world. This is what I mean by looking for the people to partner with. Many Zennials, in their eagerness to punish the financial institutions and the capitalist infrastructure that maintains them, simply advocate tearing it all to the ground. This is not practical, practicable or prudent, because it would be throwing the proverbial baby out with the bathwater.

INHABIT THE INTERSECTIONS

Alongside my career in banking, I have also spent most of my life as a mentor in the Christian Church, writing extensively on how there is more to life than just a career and how it is possible to find true existential purpose in the workplace.

I remember that when I published my first book, *God at Work*, my colleagues in those glass towers looked at me with bemusement. What is a bullish banker doing writing a book about God and spirituality? Few things seem more diametrically opposed to the things of spiritual importance than fiscal years, quarterly earning reports, and IPOs.

It is true that often these two worlds collide. But in my life, these two arenas have proved helpful in informing one another in ways beyond my imagination. They can be in tension, and in moments of real ultimatum, I've had to choose one over the other, but integration has been possible. I've experienced a similar tension when it comes to political activism.

I've been the one 'sticking it to the man' back when I was a student activist against Apartheid South Africa in the 1960s, or marching at the BLM protests in 2020. But equally, I was 'the establishment' Boomer back when thousands of young people crowded in front of St Paul's cathedral in 2008 calling for the abolition of capitalism and for the metaphorical (I hope!) lynching of the bigwigs sitting up there in those banks recklessly spending their money for personal profit and gain.

At the time, when I was asked to mediate between the protestors and the City, the experience was far from peaceful. There is a kind of power, confidence and resolve that you feel being the activist. Equally, there is a kind of smallness and feeling of being misunderstood when you are on the protested side.

Again, these two experiences are diametrically opposed but both provided important insights into what it means to live in an age of great change, discontent and fear. I don't mean to come across as arrogant or blow my own trumpet, but I have lived in these difficult intersections throughout my entire life and have realized that things are slightly more complicated than I often want them to be.

It is in these intersections that the most practical, effective and actionable insights can be gained. Many of us today look to the people speaking in the 'liminal' spaces. Those in the 'in-between' spaces. They don't belong to any specific institution or world, but have gained unique insights from seeing them from the outside.

However, I contend this won't help us to create a better world. A liminal voice cannot know what it is like to actually live in those worlds. Instead, we need voices that speak from the 'intersecting' spaces – people who are fully in different worlds and have an understanding of the internal workings of multiple different arenas of society. This is what CO looks like and this is how CO will come about. This is truly working together.

I think what our world needs more than ever is 'practical wisdom' – to know what to do at the right time, with the right means. I want to do my part to temper some of the ideas that undergird the good intentions of Zennials, and also provide practical ways in which they can implement them.

As I have already said, this is a generation with foresight, which is best expressed in the belief that practical wisdom for this age can only be found by pairing the hindsight of the Boomer and the insight of the Zennial. The binocular effect works in drawing these two sights together in a unified and clearly focused way. We need to be authentically 'Janus-faced' – not in the deceptive 'two-faced' sense but in the sense of fixing our sights firmly on both the past and the future. Together, it will be a formidable force for the progress and strengthening of capitalism.

CO AND THE BOOMER–ZENNIAL SPLIT

So where do we start? From what I have said already so far in this book about Zennials – the generation set to be the beneficiaries of the Great Wealth Transfer, the generation that will change capitalism and the way we live forever – you might assume I think we're in good enough hands for the baton to be passed smoothly without any need for intervention. Yes, we have problems, but can they not be solved by Zennials alone? Well, no.

Many of my own generation do not want to see the baton passed to a group they're convinced will drop it. And many Zennials believe the baton to be no longer fit for purpose anyway. They don't want it. They'd rather see it thrown out completely. But we must preserve the baton. We must maintain the key deliverables of a market economy: incentive, performance and reward for creating value. And we must avoid an emerging neo-socialism where 'common good' is not properly defined.

For us to end up following the narrow road, the one that ends with a better capitalism, a better system that is defined by CO, generational fractures need to be mended. This will require input from both sides. Both Boomers and Zennials need to engage.

THE ART OF CO-INVESTING

Boomers need to wake up to the fact that this shift is happening. This is not just a feckless fad. Deep levels of felt disadvantage will express itself in social dislocation and anti-establishment sentiment unless addressed. We have benefited significantly in the last 60 years and it is our duty to be able to pass on our benefits to the generation below. This can take many different forms. It can look like directly supporting entrepreneurial endeavours financially. The Zennial generation are hungry and industrial – they are starters and need fresh injections of capital to help them fly. Let's call this CO-investing. For those with the means, I'd encourage you to seek out opportunities to invest in them.

It can also look like investing in them emotionally or with your expertise. The world may have changed but the basic rules of engagement remain the same. Good business will always be good business and so taking the time out of your day and offering your point of view to these young starters would be a great place to begin. I would say that investing in the Zennial generation is as good an act of charity as donating to an NGO, perhaps even better. You may feel as though the Zennials don't want your help or that they don't have the humility to accept your point of view, but from my experience, if you go with a genuine heart to help them succeed, you will be an invaluable asset. It also helps if you have some cash to hand to get some skin in the game.

To Zennials: forgive and partner. The first thing I would say to you is 'I'm sorry.' I think I've made it clear that I think you have been handed an incredibly difficult hand. I can't say Boomers are to blame for all of that, but I can say that we are responsible for some, if not most of it. Getting ahead and succeeding will be less guaranteed for you than it was for my generation. It's always been true that in any generation, there are winners and losers – some play the right cards at the wrong time, others the wrong cards at the right time – but inequality has always existed. I appreciate, however, that the intergenerational inequality of opportunity, of wealth and of influence is keenly felt by all of you.

There are many reasons why you feel justifiably hard done by, particularly financially. However, what I'd like to say to you is don't let this sense of injustice harden your heart and embitter you. Don't let the anger over one aspect of your life be the domino effect that infects with bitterness the rest of it. I have seen lots of young people – bright, intelligent and industrious young people – eaten alive by their own sense of injustice and fail to achieve their full potential.

THE NEW MANDELA EFFECT

As I grew up in South Africa, Nelson Mandela was one of my heroes. I met him on several occasions and was a trustee in the UK of his Children's Fund. After his long years in prison, he came out as a man who was a champion for reconciliation. He once said that 'bitterness is drinking poison and hoping the other person dies'. I think this applies just as much in this case of generational fracture. There will always be people who will look down on a generation different to their own and say that it is ungrateful, entitled and ignorant of what real hard work looks like. They have been embittered by their own sense of injustice with being villainized. But that isn't the important thing.

The important thing is that you rise above bitterness and above hatred and get to work with the things you care about and avoid retaliating with the same stereotyped word-knives that are being thrown at you.

If you have a soft heart and grow to have hard hands you may also find that there will be people from my generation who would absolutely love to come alongside you and help you flourish. A friend of mine, who also happens to be a leader of one of the largest private equity groups in London, was once telling me about the importance of diversity in his thinking. When I asked him what he meant by that, he explained that intergenerational diversity was one of the most important factors for successful decision making. He said that he has been humbled by how fast society has changed and the level of fluidity that defines it, which does not come naturally to a Boomer. He was insistent that having intergenerational perspectives would result in a better quality of debate, better decisions and better outcomes. He had come to that conclusion after being taken to task by a cohort of his younger executives.

There are older people who are listening to you. So let your voice be heard and let that voice be encouraging and constructive. The establishment is listening too and is trying to find a solution to the generational estrangement you may feel. It is easy to critique, but critique is always received better when multiple solutions are also put forward.

If opportunities arise, I encourage all young people to team up with Boomers. Team up with older people who have been the beneficiaries of the asset allocations. As a society, we are working longer and longer and older people still want to pursue new and exciting ventures even after retirement. Give them something to get behind. Recognize that in an economy that is changing so rapidly in its fundamental nature, what seems intuitive to you about the digital age will be lightning strikes of insight to a Boomer. Equally, recognize that the hindsight of the older generation can provide deep wells of wisdom concerning how to grow an organization effectively. There are opportunities for you to outstrip the established corporations of a previous generation if you combine your Zennial insight with the Boomer hindsight. So seek mentors and willing partners who will co-work with you. Those who are willing to have skin in your game and want you to succeed. This may be a privilege that is not open to everyone, but if the opportunity does arise, do not turn it down to go it alone.

Because that is the main danger here. That the generation about to inherit the money, power and influence that will shape the next century feel that their best option is to go it alone. That is the antithesis of CO.

That is why I have written this book. To offer some guidance to both Boomers and Zennials for how to navigate the oncoming shift effectively. I mentioned earlier that many Zennials have an iconoclastic view of the global market economy. There are many who are anticipating the decline in influence of Boomers with a perverse glee because, with the gatekeepers gone, they will finally be able to burn the whole system to the ground. I understand why this seems an attractive option. But the consequences will not be pretty and they will be borne by you, Zennials, not those you're angry at.

What is needed is a renewal. Capitalism needs a reformation led by the insights of CO-inspired Zennials and informed by the hard-earned hindsight of Boomers. Reforms are expensive and complex and lack the short-term satisfaction of a violent revolution. But they also have the potential to change things for better and forever. I believe this is achievable through CO.

In the remainder of this book we will examine how the major fractures in our society, which we have discussed so far, can be healed through adopting CO attitudes. The prevailing attitude is that the world is going to hell in a handcart, it's somebody else's fault, and there's nothing anyone can do about it. That is not what I believe.

History usually moves imperceptibly slowly. Society changes gradually, glacially even. But we now have the immense advantage of knowing that we are entering a period where change will happen very suddenly with ground-shaking consequences. This is a gift we must not ignore. The consequences will be dire if we do.

'A successful society must provide its citizens with a dream of the future.'[1] I believe we can create that dream through CO; a workable, realistic plan for how we come out the other side better off. We'll start by looking at leadership and how it needs to operate in the twenty-first century.

7

CO-Leading

When it comes to talking about CO, the notion of leadership is vital, because without some agreement over who is leading the conversation, we are guaranteed to be blown off course. The problem is that the very idea of authority and leadership has lost a huge amount of credibility and impact in today's Western world. This has major implications for the future of the Western world as we know it and the capitalism that underpins its economy.

Largely, my generation has believed that what we need are strong, clear leaders; more often than not a great, visionary figure. It's the Great Man Theory of leadership: that some are just born to rule. Napoleon, for example. Or Catherine the Great. Or Churchill. Or Alexander the Great. Or even Steve Jobs. You get the picture. The idea is that all great pursuits in society are the fruit of a great leader's vision, clarity and ability to muster action. This command-and-control management model has been steadily eroded by the changing requirements of Zennial participants in the market economy. Business schools have been at the forefront of leading the changeover from the more dirigiste model to a more collaborative one. Shared leadership, servant leadership and participative leadership have emerged as these new models.

In short, Zennials have a different point of view when it comes to leadership. (It will not be a 'great person' that leads us to CO.) For Zennials, good leadership is fundamentally collaborative and decentralized: after all, we've had countless leaders fail us – this is particularly true in the corporate world. There is not a single sphere of our lives where these apparently great leaders have not failed us in some shape or form. Technology and social media have proved that there are ways to organize mass collective action without the need for a leader with centralized power. The best kind of authority is when everyone has a slice. This does sound like a far more compelling vision of leadership – indeed, it's safeguarded from all the abuses of power that we have, sadly, come to expect from our leaders. However, it's important to recognize that this posture is still a reaction to the fractures in our relationship to authority and leaders.

THE FRACTURE OF LEADERSHIP

As we have discussed previously, trust in financial and other institutions, governments, media and religious leaders has hit an all-time low. Indeed, *distrust* as the status quo is now fairly well established. It is the default setting of a generation.

'Nearly 6 in 10 say their default tendency is to distrust something until they see evidence it is trustworthy. Another 64% say it's now to a point where people are incapable of having constructive and civil debates about issues they disagree on. When distrust is the default – we lack the ability to debate or collaborate.'[1] That's one of the key conclusions from the 2022 Edelman Trust Barometer.

Trust in leadership is crucial to CO, so these divisions need to be mended. The key institutions that we take our lead from aren't about to change, so they will need to prioritize the building of trust at every level of the organization if they are to engage productively with the emerging CO generation.

These trends are universal, particularly in the West. There is a significant level of cynicism in our leaders, institutions and anything that claims a level of universal authority. The last several years has aggravated this trend, but it has been a trend that's been on the agenda for the last several decades. And this has resulted in two different competing visions of what 'authority' should look like, and its role in our life together.

A few years ago, I attended a conference in New York on inclusive capitalism. It was based on how we could make the market economy work for a new generation. The whole conference was about how we could make the free market more inclusive so that more people could reap the benefits of compound interest and stable wealth growth and generation, particularly more inclusive to a generation who have grown up in a particularly chaotic time for the financial markets. Throughout the day, there was one acronym that was used over and over again to describe the times we live in, and that was VUCA.

Volatile.
Uncertain.
Complex.
Angry.

It perfectly describes our moment. And it is against this backdrop that the new Zennial worldview has been formed. It seems as though, every day, we are entering an increasingly VUCA world. Pandemic aside, geo-political relations across key global powers such as America, China and Russia are at a level of precariousness not seen in decades, each vying to outmanoeuvre the other at the potential cost of destabilizing the delicate global economy and network of supply chains.

Alongside this, the project of the internet seems to be fragmenting along these geo-political lines. I remember when the internet was first introduced and there was so much vision and hope for what it could become. Back in 1996, a manifesto was put forward called 'A Declaration of the Independence of Cyberspace',[2] penned by John Perry Barlow, a founder of the Electronic Frontier Foundation. It described the internet as a potential game-changer that could catalyse a movement towards an ungoverned, utopic, global society that couldn't be stifled by various nation-states – or the 'weary giants of flesh and steel'. The internet would give power to the people, and we would rise above the traditional boundaries that separated humanity for so long.

It's worth looking at the opening in full:

Governments of the Industrial World, you weary giants of flesh and steel, I come from Cyberspace, the new home of Mind. On behalf of the future, I ask you of the past to leave us alone. You are not welcome among us. You have no sovereignty where we gather.

We have no elected government, nor are we likely to have one, so I address you with no greater authority than that with which liberty itself always speaks. I declare the global social space we are building to be naturally independent of the tyrannies you seek to impose on us. You have no moral right to rule us nor do you possess any methods of enforcement we have true reason to fear.

Looking back on it, it's wonderfully, if naively, idealistic. Because this is not what the internet has become, is it? It is not independent of tyranny. Indeed, Big Tech has become tyrannical in ways most of us never could have predicted despite its own idealistic beginnings.

The *Financial Times*'s Rana Foroohar has written a book on how Big Tech has betrayed its founding principles and she opens it like this:

'Don't be evil' is the famous first line of Google's original Code of Conduct, what seems today like a quaint relic of the company's early days, when the crayon colours of the Google logo still conveyed the cheerful, idealistic spirit of the enterprise. How long ago that feels. Of course, it would be unfair to accuse Google of being actively evil. But evil is as evil does, and some of the things that Google and other Big Tech firms have done in recent years have not been very nice.[3]

Well, quite. The dream of the internet hasn't been as expected.

And today, it now seems that those 'weary giants of flesh and steel' Barlow addressed are working together with Big Tech to construct national borders within the internet. The great firewall of China and the digital ecosystems that companies like WeChat and Alipay uphold have already created a walled garden called the 'Internet of China'. A similar movement is occurring in Russia, their local tech companies such as Yandex and Mail.ru that dominate their markets providing a whole local ecosystem with unique search engines, counterparts to Facebook and Twitter, and Google internet services. You can be a citizen in China and Russia today and not have to engage at all with Google, Facebook or Netflix and still experience the full benefit of digital services available to us in the UK. Even the internet, which was once a very 'simple' democratic, global space, without a necessary leader, has become a VUCA environment.

Combine these with the ongoing fallout of trust from the Global Financial Crisis, huge scandals involving our politicians and business leaders, the handling of global terrorism, the seeming rise of populist leaders, the outing of sexual harassment in almost every industry, and there is a palpable sense that things have not quite gone to plan. The world did not become a global utopia, the internet did not set us free, and the leaders, institutions and structures that seemed so stable were revealed to be very fragile indeed.

Perhaps one of the most defining emotions that a Zennial feels is the sense that they have been failed by the people they ought to have trusted – their leaders – and they are angry.

ANXIOUS FOLLOWERS

On reflection, I would add an additional 'A' to VUCA – VUCAA if you will. 'A' for anxiety. The state of the world is one that is causing severe anxiety to the Zennial and this is evident in every workplace. The sand is shifting below their feet on a daily basis and they are anxious in an unsettled world, be it in the micro or the macro. How do I live in this kind of world? What is my purpose and place? How do I know anything I stand on will last? This needs to be a consideration of corporations, which need to offer avenues to their employees to help them deal with this anxiety.

This zeitgeist was captured well by Andy Beckett, who wrote in the *Guardian* that the 2010s will be remembered as one of 'Perpetual Crisis':

> During the 2010s, there have been crises of democracy and the economy; of the climate and poverty; of international relations and national identity; of privacy and technology. There were crises at the start of the decade, and there are crises now. Some of them are the same crises, unsolved. Others are like nothing we have experienced before.[4]

And Zennials have attributed the sense of perpetual crisis to the failure of institutions and leaders. In fact, in Deloitte's 2019 Global Millennial Survey it was found that nearly three-quarters (73 per cent) said that political leaders are failing to have a positive impact on the world. Two-thirds say the same about faith leaders. This is a huge indictment of my generation. Regardless of the objective truth of the claim, the fact that the perception of leaders has hit rock bottom is something to take note of.

This statistic is beautifully coloured in by the lyrics of Australian artist Tones and I's 2019 single 'The kids are coming'.

The lyrics of another Zennial pop sensation, Olivia Rodrigo, serve to illustrate much better than I could the point I made above about anxiety in this generation. Her debut album, *SOUR*, was released in 2021, when she was 18, and the opening track, 'Brutal' depicts this anxiety so well with lines like 'And I'm so caught up in the news of who likes me, and who hates you'.

At this point, it is important to note that the objective reality about whether the world is getting worse or not is less relevant than the felt experience of the generation living it. Max Roser, the Oxford economist behind the website 'Our World in Data', has pointed out that any newspaper publication could legitimately have published the headline 'NUMBER OF PEOPLE IN EXTREME POVERTY FELL BY 137,000 SINCE YESTERDAY' every day for the last 25 years. Author Yuval Noah Harari and other 'New Optimists' are quick to point out that we live in the most prosperous, healthiest, most peaceful time in human history. Swedish author Johan Norberg points out that as recently as 1882, only 2 per cent of homes in New York had running water; in 1900, worldwide life expectancy was 31 years old, thanks both to early adult death and rampant child mortality (no Boomers in those days I suppose). The world, according to these optimists, has never been better and it is simply the emotive, uninformed and click-bait-driven newsrooms that are driving a global pessimism.

Despite the legitimacy of these positions, it fails to recognize that the perception of the Zennial generation is not merely a matter of numbers and statistics. The deep emotions they feel are connected not so much to the general progress of society as to the specific loss of faith and trust in their Boomer counterparts in finance and politics who were meant to lead them.

LOOKING FOR A GREAT PERSON ALTERNATIVE

These failures of leadership and institution have dethroned one of the great myths of our world: that Great Man Theory, the nineteenth-century idea according to which history can be largely explained by the impact of great men (because it was always men back then), or heroes; highly influential and unique individuals who, due to their natural attributes, such as superior intellect, heroic courage or divine inspiration, had a decisive historical effect.

We see this myth reflected in all sorts of places. We often talk, for example, about inspired creative geniuses and heroes. Steve Jobs, who single-handedly changed what it means to be human with his iPhone; Martin Luther King and Nelson Mandela, who were linchpins in racial healing throughout the world; or Winston Churchill, who seemingly by the strength of his will led the Allies to victory. It is the traditional way we think about the word 'leader', associating it with a single figure – the CEO, the head of government, the Chair of the Board.

However Zennials are beginning to change the old rules of leadership. We are now moving into the age of the CO-leader. As I mentioned earlier, we are entering the era of 'take me to your network' rather than 'take me to your leader'. The era of command-and-control leadership has gone. More than that, we have moved into a world of collegiate leadership. CO is not merely a title when the institution can't make a decision of who to appoint and then appoints co-CEOs for example. Shared experience and learning become the hallmark of a new CO-leadership ethos. CO-leading changes our notion of what a leader is. Rather than being omnipotent and autocratic, this new type of CO leader – or, more specifically, leaders – calls for humility, inclusivity and empathy. Even as Zennials have navigated the workplace and stepped into leadership positions, they have demanded accessibility regardless of title, with less emphasis on company hierarchies and more emphasis on transparency, inclusivity and core competences. There has been a significant movement towards 'mutual collaboration' over and above good leadership.

These stipulations have led to CO-leadership, an authority ideal that now needs to be embraced by all. CO-leadership means harnessing the talents of the entire enterprise and incorporating people at all different levels. CO-leadership means dismantling corrupt power structures and, in doing so, creating safer work environments. The particularly contemporary twist is that leadership today has to be through networks. Digital technology enables us to find, share and develop information together to a degree never possible before. As CO leaders, we must understand the power of networks and how to use them. If we do not, our voices will go unheeded and our enterprises will fail. At the base level, this recognizes the contribution of experience and worldly wisdom as well as the ceaseless innovative capacity of Zennials to shape their world.

CO-LEADING IN ACTION

Some of the most influential and important social movements of the twenty-first century have not had a heroic great individual leader, be it the Arab Spring, Occupy Wall Street, the Umbrella Revolution in Hong Kong, or Black Lives Matter movements. In all these movements, while spokespeople have come in and out of the scene, there has not been a consolidated single leader to galvanize the movement and yet they have touched more people than any of the previous movements of the last 100 years.

Greta Thunberg, while an icon and a hero of her generation, cannot be said to be the leader of Extinction Rebellion; Joshua Wong, the student activist in Hong Kong who has been imprisoned multiple times and has been a key voice and advocate in the fight for democracy against China, does not 'lead' the Umbrella Revolution in any meaningful way. The current protests in Iran at the time of writing, particularly those sparked after the killing of Mahsa Amini, do not have an obvious and vocal individual leader. Protests are organized organically through messaging services such as Telegram and information is disseminated via the digital superhighway. In fact, today, you don't even need to be in the country to organize mass protests.

In late July and August of 2020, the country of Belarus became unrecognizable as hundreds of thousands of pro-democracy protestors took to the streets against the long-standing President Alexander Lukashenko. Lukashenko has led the country since 1996 and he had won another, supposedly 'democratic', election in 2020. In an incredible feat of mass collaboration and coordination, rivalling Hong Kong's pro-democracy protests, protestors marched down the streets of central Minsk, as well as the broadways of smaller towns like Brest, Gomel or Khotsimsk, carrying placards and waving the traditional Belarussian flag of independence.

However, unlike in Hong Kong, the protests were not organized by local, young students on the ground with the protestors. Rather, the bulk of the mass coordination was organized by a 22-year-old blogger called Stsiapan Sviatlou, who lives outside the country and runs a channel called NEXTA Live on the social messaging platform Telegram. His not being within the Belarussian border allowed him to rouse the population with messages and manifestos without fearing the scrutiny and censorship of the government. He was able to publish patriotic videos and commentary without fear of arrest, and so could reach millions of people at the most intimate level: through their smartphones. In generations past, the voice in the public square resounded in the hearts of people. Today, the public square is digital, and it doesn't need an open-air megaphone to capture hearts and minds.

As *Atlantic* journalist Anne Applebaum observes:

[P]eople all across Belarus have marched, protested, carried red and white flags and banners, and gathered at factories and outside prisons because they trust what they read on Nexta. They trust Nexta even though Sviatlou is only 22 years old, even though he is an amateur blogger, and even though he is outside the country.

Or to put it more accurately, they trust Nexta *because* Sviatlou is only 22, and because he is an amateur who lives outside the country. In Belarus, the government is a kind of presidential monarchy with no checks, no balances, and no rule of law ...

They don't trust the government, they can't hear the opposition – but more than 2 million people subscribe to the Nexta Live channel, and hundreds of thousands more follow Sviatlou on YouTube, Instagram, and Twitter, as well as his other Telegram channels, because they trust him. And no wonder: He shows them pictures of people like themselves. He shows them videos of places they recognize. His public persona is optimistic, idealistic, and patriotic. In photographs, he is usually smiling. Plus, he is in Poland, a place where police can't get the data on his telephone, so it is safe to read what he writes and to send him information.[5]

Sviatlou is not a traditional leader. He was not a political opponent to Lukashenko, he didn't give rousing speeches or stand on the front line of the protests. His gift is curating collaboration, and it is this skill that has made the difference in the twenty-first century. He is a curator, not only a creator. It is easy to dismiss these as political protests but it's a new paradigm and soon such protests will be directed on a similar scale against corporations. The way they will be responded to will indicate the level of co-understanding that exists between the C-suite and the unseen blogger.

A NEW EMPHASIS IN LEADERSHIP

When reflecting on all this, I am reminded of the military concept of 'co-belligerence'. This refers to waging a war against a common enemy without a formal treaty of military alliance. Ukraine is a current example of a coalition of co-belligerents supporting its response to Russia. Military support in this case may refer to material goods, exchanging intelligence, and some limited operational coordination. However, the motivations for war on either side of the co-belligerent partnership are likely to be quite different. They could include cultural, religious or ideological differences (as compared to an 'alliance', which implies an ideological or motivational closeness). Different sides come together to fight for a common cause even if these sides are radically opposed in other ways. It really is true that nothing unites better than a common enemy.

Is mass support of particular protest movements the Zennial equivalent of co-belligerence? It could well be the case that, as proprietary ownership of movements is no longer dominant (thanks to technology increasing connection, and so forth), members of protest/ideological movement groups are prepared to cede principle for direction. This would seem to signal the end of an emphasis on strong leadership. Instead, it signals a time when 'The Big Idea' is taken far more seriously, and where we value the ideas as outliving the people who are behind them. This has major implications for the corporate world, because it will shape strategic thinking in every organization as Zennials look to bring fresh thinking and differing perspectives to the fore. No decision-making structure will flourish if it does not actively co-opt Zennial executives into the discussions on future strategy and growth.

Where is the Martin Luther King of this generation? Should we lament the fact that there isn't one? Or is it perhaps the case that the sort of leadership that defined the Civil Rights movement against the Jim Crow laws no longer applies to our CO world? Such movements can outlast a charismatic leader – and surely that is a good thing. If an alien were to visit us, they might say: 'Take me to your leader.' And we might reply: 'We'll take you to our network.'

But why is CO-leadership not necessarily working?

While many contemporary protest movements demonstrate the incredible efficacy and power of a generation in which leadership is decentralized, they demonstrate the catastrophic failures of them also.

Black Lives Matter is a particularly interesting example. It is a leading instance of the new CO world in action, namely a new form of community made possible by digital means. However, it has also proved to be one of the most controversial campaign groups of our time. Regularly cited by supporters and opponents on each side of the culture wars, the campaign has unfortunately come to symbolize a divided nation, and a divided world. Unity and reconciliation – indeed, true healing and understanding – appear further away than ever. Public discourse is becoming more polarized, not less. Why is this the case? Wasn't it the Great Men leaders who caused division with their petty fights? Haven't we sought to democratize and decentralize authority? Isn't mutual collaboration our main *modus operandi*? And how is it that the greatest countries in the world have, at least until recently, actually been run by the most archetypal Great Men leaders, be it Donald Trump, Xi in China, or Putin in Russia?

As with many things, the great advantage of mutual collaboration – its democratized, flat structure and permeability of power and leadership – is also its great disadvantage. Traditionally, a leader was the person who would provide the common vision and voice of any movement or organization. They would be the arbiter of what was going 'too far' and would speak for the movement when engaging with opposing bodies. A movement without a clear leader or authority structure does not have this advantage. The arbiter is the collective, and voices that would never have been amplified in any previous generation are now being augmented based on popular provocation, rather than on merit and reasonableness. A movement run by the people for the people can quickly turn into a mob. The shadow side of collaboration is populism or tribalism.

Zennials will be heard and will use financial power, influence and technology to ensure that the concerns expressed in society as a whole also shape the capital markets. Refusing capital to those who do not subscribe to the prevailing ethos will be a regrettable but inevitable outcome unless the principles of CO are realized.

THE THREAT OF TRIBALISM

In the early days of the internet, there was a saying doing the rounds attributed to IBM and AT&T veteran Jim Barksdale about the great changes that were taking place in tech and the information age. He said that 'there are only two ways I know to make money; bundling or unbundling'. He was talking about the revolutionary changes taking place in the media business at the start of the internet information age. There was a great unbundling taking place, which was changing the face of the music and video industry forever. Unbundling is what happens when you can begin to sell parts of things that only used to be able to be bought as a whole.

Music has been a great example of unbundling. With the rise of the MP3 marketplace, CDs became unbundled – you could just buy the song you loved and not have to pay £7.99 for an album. Similarly, print newspapers became unbundled as Facebook and Google's aggregators made purchasing a whole edition each day obsolete. Why would you buy a paper in the morning, when you could have your news stories in real time published 24/7?

TV has had a serious run of unbundling, with internet streaming services slowly but surely driving people to cut the cord with their TV providers and start paying marginal prices for more specialized services. I remember a time when I was purchasing my Sky TV bundle. I bought a package and there was so much I didn't need from it. One bundle would give me live sports, movies, cartoons, God TV, Disney, history documentaries and hundreds of other channels when all I really wanted was the news and good drama shows. Internet unbundling put an end to that. Entertainment itself was unbundled into different corners of the internet. As one commentator put it so well: 'information going to Google, education to YouTube, story-telling to streaming, and escapism to everything from TikTok to video games to Netflix'.

During the 1990s and early 2000s, there seemed to be a great unbundling not only in the media consumption sphere, but also in the socio-political sphere. This era was really a time of unbundled politics. It was the era of centrist leaders who unbundled traditional left- and right-wing policies, whether the New Labour of Tony Blair, or the formidable coalition that Angela Merkel secured in Germany. Even in China and Russia, after the dissolution of the Soviet Union, centrist politics took the stage, with most governments embracing some form of free-market capitalism and financial principles. Both Boris Yeltsin of Russia and Jiang Zemin of China knew they needed economic reforms that aligned their respective countries along the lines of the global free market.

Culture was unbundled from economics, which was unbundled from national pride and social policy. In short, ideologies were unbundled. Buying into one type of economics did not commit you to anything else, be it your opinion on social housing, abortion or an interpretation of a nation's history. However, if Barksdale is to be believed, when everything becomes unbundled, there is only one way to make money. Start bundling again.

Streaming services facilitated the great unbundling of TV but we are already seeing a great rebundling. Disney has begun the rebundling of internet TV as it aggressively acquires live sports channels such as ESPN, television and film studios like 20th Century Fox, and documentary powerhouses like National Geographic, offering their customers the full suite of television programming, just like the old TV providers used to. Amazon is following suit as it aggressively partners with the Premier League and the ATP Tour to offer live sports to their consumers. YouTube has been doing the same, expanding its offerings to movie rentals and live TV subscriptions. You can no longer buy a single channel, but have to buy into the package, and you can't negotiate the contents of the package. Buy Disney, and you will end up with National Geographic, Marvel Superheroes and Fox. And it seems that we are seeing a rebundling in the socio-political world as well. A bundled socio-economic, political and moral vision of the world is what we could otherwise call aggressive tribalism. It is this tribalism, when energized by an empowered generation, that needs urgent dismantling if the market economy is to survive fit for purpose, for that next generation.

We humans love to form tribes and groups. In an age when the socio-political balance of the world is being rocked and competing visions of the future are being articulated globally we form strong loyalties to our groups and to our communities. And as we form those strong group connections, we are rediscovering the power of collective action. We are being asked to swear our allegiance to different groups all the time. The Zennial knows that they must stand for something, they can't remain on the sidelines and be an observer. You have to choose. It didn't necessarily used to be like this. Indeed, individualism reigned supreme for a long time. Committing to a collective, identifying with a cause, was not a requirement.

But recognizing that radical individualism is not a tenable way forward has meant that you have to start thinking of yourself as part of a group in order to participate properly in the issues of our day. Once we start creating these groups, and swear our allegiance to them, then of course we become deeply invested in making sure that our group triumphs over others, no matter the cost. As Jonathan Haidt observes, 'our politics is groupish, not selfish'. And our world today is prime time for groupishness. This is most obvious in the partisan politics of the US. There are only two realistic packages you can buy. One package means you have to embrace small government, pro-life, pro-gun, evangelical nationalism; and the other means you have to embrace large government, pro-choice, anti-gun, secular globalism. It doesn't seem like a fair choice any more, but those are the tribal identities that have formed, so you had better choose one. And it seems that tribalism and groupishness is increasing by the year.

We are trapped in silos after the great rebundling of politics that are preventing us from having any kind of inter-tribe dialogues, and this is incredibly dangerous. Because of this all-or-nothing approach, the prevailing idea is that we must disagree on everything with those who hold opposing views to us. This is not sustainable. We cannot become further entrenched. We need to rediscover the ability to have unbundled views. To be able to have conversations in which nuance is considered. Where one person's view on a single issue doesn't immediately leave them branded as a bigot or a snowflake.

These silos that we find ourselves in are one of the key roadblocks to the necessary intergenerational cooperation that is required if we are to build a new capitalism together. Because of the prevailing tribal attitudes, assumptions are made about people's views simply on the basis of their age, and conversation is not allowed to flow between the generations because Boomers have already made up their minds about Zennials, and vice versa. I know from experience that this does not need to be our reality. As we have already discussed, we will all benefit by simply understanding that, while we may disagree in some areas, we can make a much greater impact by working together.

CO-LEADING IS NOT COLLECTIVISM

There was a presumption not too long ago that the only viable system of economics and governance was the Western free market. It brought unprecedented wealth and development to the world and seemed like it was going to continue that way forever. However, that assumption has seen significant challenges through the 2010s. As divisions in the West widen with increased polarization of social and moral convictions, China's apparent success and newfound, albeit dirigiste, confidence has illuminated the West's doubts about itself. Indeed, democratization remains unfinished business so long as two of the world's biggest countries – China and Russia – are potential authoritarian magnets. Globalization, meanwhile, has poured fuel on the flames. Clashes of values are responsible for a lot of the tensions of globalization. There is a widespread resentment at what is regarded in many parts of the emerging world such as Asia and Latin America as the imposition of a Western, and specifically American, culture under the guise of free trade and intellectual property rights – what was revealingly styled the 'Washington Consensus'.

Even where the benefits of global trade and the market economy are seen and appreciated, the yearning to protect local custom and practice, and their accompanying values, has been strong. Real passions lie just below the surface, with developing countries deeply resenting being lectured on the urgency of moving to a low-carbon economy by rich countries whose prosperity was built on profligate burning of fossil fuels.

While multilateral, collaborative methods of working naturally leads to increased permeability of goods and values, these have the counter effect of watering down the cultural vibrancy that humans desperately seek. Billions of people all over the world cherish their own history, institutions and ways of life. Africans, Brazilians, Chinese and Indians are forging their own futures, drawing on their own cultures and values while rejecting previous theories of development in isolation and choosing to participate in the global economy. As these and other emerging market economies expand, they will export their values with their products and practices and grow more confident about asserting those values.

The future of globalization and civil life depends to a considerable degree on reconciling all these competing values on a mutually agreed basis, and reconciling the different visions of justice, goodness and society that permeate our world today. This may be the challenge of our day, but it is currently felt as schisms and fractures. It is the most keenly felt reality. Whether you are in the US, or the UK, or in Turkey, or Brazil, the level of polarization of society on party and community lines is becoming seismic. Visions of the 2016 US election, Brexit referendum, failed military coups, and pro-democracy mass protests come to mind, and the claim that our world is becoming more collaborative and 'together' seems naive and counterintuitive.

And this is where it is so important to distinguish between 'collectivism' and CO. As we have seen, collectivism eradicates the individual in favour of the group ideal; it's the kind of thinking that can lead to the Soviet famines of the 1930s where millions of people were left to starve in Ukraine and beyond because what is the value of millions when it can serve the billions of the future in the glorious communist world? Collectivism doesn't recognize the infinite value and worth of the individual and is willing to sacrifice them for the 'greater' good – humans become less valuable than ideas in collectivism. And this is the temptation of the radical collaboration we are seeing today.

Zennials are passionate and deeply resonate with ideas and ideals that will change the world, and can leverage extraordinary collaborative action to actually move the needle. They can mobilize hundreds of thousands, if not millions of people globally to advocate for a cause on the other side of the world – it is truly extraordinary. However, as they do this, it is important that they do not slide into radical collectivism.

If we begin sliding into collectivism, it ironically opens the door to the return of 'Strong Man' leaders – people who will take advantage of the perceived chaos, exploit the diminished role that individuals play in a collectivist movement, and wield the collective energy to their own ends. Indeed, this trend is already being seen throughout the world in the rise of new populist movements. Basically, be careful what you wish for.

HEALING AUTHORITY

I understand the Zennial cynicism towards power, authority and leaders. We have had appalling examples of the highest order, from corruption to embezzling. No greater evil has come to light than the wickedness of child abuse, which has destroyed a generation's trust in institutions ranging from the BBC, the army, the Church, the media, FIFA and politics. There isn't a single institution or position of authority that has not been tainted in some way.

However, every experiment to abolish hierarchy has been met with the same results as dismissing the law of gravity.

Attempt to fly unaided and gravity will reassert itself very quickly, with potentially dire consequences. There will always be hierarchies that will emerge among groups of people. There will be the charismatic speaker, or the gruff army general, or the Machiavellian who will be able to gather people around them for better or for worse. We will not abolish the human truth that natural born leaders exist, or that some people will be opportunistic when there is a vacuum of power. No other leadership experiment can take its place.

The answer, however, is not to abolish authority, but to fix authority. Learn how to listen and how to disagree well. Not every use of power is an abuse of power. We can demand more good from our leaders and also watch out for signs of bad leadership. Over the years, I have seen great leaders forge a new future, and have come across those who have ruined the lives of their employees and followers.

Beware of leaders who stop listening to the little guy. I have come across far too many whose success has inflated their egos to the point of megalomania. They are overconfident and feel as though they know every answer to every question. They may very well be incredibly competent and smart, but leaders who shut themselves into a world of their own are on a one-track road to a crash that will destroy either them or, more likely, the people around them. Often, these leaders will make brash decisions off their own bat, confident in their own ability. We tend to believe that a good leader is one who makes good decisions. However, the process of decision making is just as important as the decision itself. And so beware of those leaders who short-cut consultation. We should not celebrate leaders for making quick decisions; instead, we should value those who make good decisions with the right people around them, even the little guy.

Beware radical collectivists. Ordinarily, we champion those visionary leaders who can step back and see the full picture and communicate a clarity of vision. However, beware those leaders who cannot see the wood for the trees. Those leaders who are so concerned with the 'big picture' and the 'mass movement' that they forget about the individual right in front of them. Often, these leaders are very charismatic and compelling, and can capture the human heart in a way a bureaucrat just can't. But if they do not pair their clarity of vision with an empathy for individuals, they will be the type of leader who will later be willing to let the 'little guys' sacrifice themselves for the 'cause'.

What Zennials have right is that our leaders need to do better. But we don't have to throw out leadership because of lots of bad leaders. We can reimagine new qualities for our leaders, and keep them accountable to them. One of the most important things that has emerged in the last 30 years is the need for transparency from our leaders. Transparency in their decision making, in their mistakes, and sometimes in their moral character. Transparency should be viewed as one of the hallmarks of good leadership in tomorrow's world, just as being a visionary, or having strong communication skills, is a hallmark of good leadership. CO-leading requires transparency as the antidote to corruption. We need to build transparent authority structures, and not be filled with fear of disclosure. It has become a home truth that it's the cover-up, not the original issue that takes an executive down. To realize these new visions of authority we need to incentivize our future leaders to be more transparent, and this puts a responsibility on all of us. Leaders will only become more transparent if we allow them space to do so. There is a responsibility on us to refrain from crucifying our leaders when they are transparent and admit to their mistakes. Too often, leaders are not incentivized to show any weakness or errors because they fear not only public scrutiny but public humiliation. There is a responsibility on the leader to bear the consequences of their mistakes, but there is also a responsibility on us to make sure that the social consequences and fallout from those mistakes are appropriate and generous.

I have hope that the Zennials will not repeat the tragic histories of the twentieth century. Save for a few radicals across the board who seem to carry a large share of voice in the media, I do see in Zennial entrepreneurs and workers a desire for actual community and genuine collaboration. A desire to share stories and values from different worldviews and to gain an understanding of a plurality of ways of seeing the world. Mutual respect, and the recognition that an opposing group is made up of real individuals with the same emotional depth as oneself, is something I see cultivated well in many of the young people I have mentored and I pray that this will be the mark of the generation. One that will learn to collaborate in a pluralistic world where consensus is achieved not by all participants sharing one culture or worldview, but through mutual understanding and sharing of knowledge and insight. Being CO-workers and CO-leaders together is the key, not sliding into inhumane collectivism or shallow individualism. It is the fusing together of the new, emerging agenda with the tried-and-tested template of the past. The fusing of the hindsight of the Boomer and the insight of the Zennial.

8

CO-WORKING

If CO-leading is the macro side of developing a capitalism in which we can live well together, CO-working is the micro. The nitty-gritty. The actual nuts and bolts of how we repair and reform effectively so that we can navigate the shifts that are approaching. On a very obvious level, learning – or rather re-learning; we do know how to do it – how to work well together will help temper the animosity that has arisen between Zennials and Boomers.

But it will also play a major role in repairing the other fissures we discussed in the first half of this book. Establishing a new way of working together will underpin the new capitalism that is needed for the challenges ahead. Embracing the side of technology that helps to unite us in ways we never could have done before will assist us in rejecting the dark side of tech that drives us apart. And then, of course, by being true CO workers, we can rebuild the communities that have been splintered. CO-working is the way out of our silos.

And CO-working is not merely about how we work together, or even where we do it – whether office or home or other creative spaces. It's also about the who: how we form corporations and organizations and teams that have the right make-up of people to benefit the whole in the most effective way, both in the sense of creating profit and of creating a better world. And it involves, too, the when of CO-working. The flexibility of the modern workplace has changed traditional business hours. How do we adapt to that most effectively?

THE NEW WORKPLACE

For the majority of my career, hierarchy has been deeply embedded into every organization and company I've worked at. In the heyday of the 1980s banking world we, on the whole, weren't all that concerned as to whether what we were doing was meaningful; we were more concerned with making money. As a career financier, I was steeped in a culture of elitism and individualism. 'Climb the ladder or get stepped on'; that was the mantra of office life. And it wasn't true just of my industry either. Many of us who were in the early days of our careers in the 1980s could attest to the realities we faced. Wellness or mental health were not meaningful concerns for employers at that time. Just incentivize people to work hard for you and not leave, and pay them well of course. We were far more willing to accept the hierarchy knowing that if we played our cards right, we would end up on top eventually and reap the benefits of this. So we were in the office every day, although sometimes resorting to subterfuge by hanging our suit jackets on desk chairs while slipping away, leaving others with the impression that we were hard at work.

Zennials don't buy this.

Workplaces today, particularly in newer organizations, are radically flat and cooperative. Out are the days of private cubicles and offices – often personalized with photographs and 'tombstones' of previous deals. In are the days of open-plan sofas and collaborative hot-desks. In fact, I know several peers in large London consultancy firms who are in the throes of crisis as the organization moves towards such co-working collaborative spaces. What to do when you're stripped of your office and have to work in the 'communal spaces'? Nothing more graphically underlines the changes in the workplace than the physical metamorphosis of these spaces. It reflects the changing shape of work in the twenty-first century, with the shift from *me* to *we* perfectly encapsulated.

As we have seen, Zennials don't like hierarchy or strict structures of authority. According to the *Harvard Business Review*, this new CO-oriented style of offices creates a greater sense of meaning, job control and community. This isn't just down to a particular product or table layout, or being given more choice over your seat. It's down to the value systems these democratized spaces try to promote. An extract from the coworkingmanifesto.com articulates this further[1]:

In order to create a sustainable community based on trust, we value:

- collaboration over competition
- community over agendas
- participation over observation
- doing over saying
- friendship over formality
- boldness over assurance
- learning over expertise
- people over personalities
- 'value ecosystem' over 'value chain'.

The principle here is clear: that the traditional 'dog eat dog' – 'survival of the fittest' – approach to working environments, previously believed to improve productivity and effectiveness, is being rejected. The very first principle is 'collaboration over competition' and this is a striking departure from the world in which I started my career.

THE WFH EFFECT

There has also, of course, in the last few years been a striking change to the way we *all*, or at least most of us, work, due to Covid. Working from home, or remote working, was a pretty niche activity before 2020. It was an occasional, once-or-twice-a-year phenomenon for most people, made necessary by a childcare emergency or perhaps the need to wait in all day for a plumber. Pre-Covid, flexible working was offered to employees as a perk, often in an attempt to attract those with young children into the workplace. Now it is a right for all and no business exists without the recognition of this right.

Statistics from the US show that, before the pandemic, only 6 per cent of the employed population worked primarily from home and about three-quarters of workers had never worked from home at all. The expectation after the pandemic, though, was that more flexible remote work opportunities would be permanently implemented.[2] That, it seems, has indeed come to pass.

The UK's Office for National Statistics reported in May 2022 that 'most people who took up home-working because of the pandemic plan to both work from home and in the workplace ("hybrid work") in the future'.[3] The working from home trend seems to have passed its peak[4] as the Covid lockdowns slowly disappear in the rear-view mirror, but the chances of working life ever returning to how it was pre-pandemic are close to nil. Workers – and remember the workforce is now dominated by Zennials – expect some form of flexibility at the very least. Companies that require in-office attendance nine to five, Monday to Friday, simply will not be able to attract the best candidates.

Even investment banks are adapting in an attempt to make sure they are an attractive proposition for Zennials. Citigroup has opened a new hub for junior staff in their twenties in the seaside city of Malaga, on Spain's Costa del Sol,[5] and has promised that, in contrast to the traditionally long hours associated with the industry, staff in Malaga will only have eight-hour days with no weekend work. Their salaries have been adjusted accordingly to around half of the $100,000 (£86,000) starting salary offered for the same roles in London and New York. But 3,000 people applied for the 30 spots available. Manolo Falcó, the bank's global co-head of banking, capital markets and advisory, said of the initiative[6]: 'Low levels of junior banker retention are being seen across the industry, and the message is clear: the key driver behind many junior-level departures is the search for a better work–life balance. At Citi, we are listening.'

Young people are demanding change to the way we work in our capitalist society and corporations are responding as necessary. The fact is that the borders between home and work have been blurred over the last few years. As well as working from home we are also living at work. Flexible working means that the demarcation between when you are on the clock and when you are off the clock has disappeared. Organizations need to respond to this by ensuring their employees have the work–life balance they crave. Otherwise, their employees will simply quit.

We are in the midst of the Great Resignation, a term coined in May 2021 to describe the record number of people leaving their jobs since the beginning of the pandemic. After an extended period of working from home with no commute, lots of people, particularly the young, have decided their work–life balance has become more important to them.[7] Because there is choice out there for Zennials. And they have nothing like the kind of loyalty to corporations that Boomers had. Boomers put a premium on job security, but Zennials like the idea of variety and are not necessarily overly concerned about moving jobs every couple of years. However, this does not mean that Zennials will not stay at a company long term under the right circumstances. A *Forbes* article[8] from 2016, talking about Millennials, summed it up as: 'They want to find a place where they feel they fit in, belong, and can make a commitment. They want to find a place with a shared purpose, shared values, and a shared mission. They want to find a place where they can be awesome.'

This is having a major impact on the way we work in the 2020s and how we will work in the remainder of the century. There is a silent, but seismic, redefinition of work emerging. According to the McKinsey Global Institute, remote work will increase productivity in the West by 1 per cent annually until 2024. The great resignation is starting to shift labour forces, integrating youthful aspirations into a new, revitalized future of work, and technology may help companies adapt to new visions of working. Companies like Meta, Cisco and Microsoft, joined by a flock of new startups, are convening virtual boardrooms. Telemedicine has now become the norm, allowing new models of more inclusive and potentially more effective holistic healthcare. Virtual reality-augmented skill-acquisition – from learning appendectomy to hospitality – has become a multibillion-dollar industry.

The questions and opportunities that arise from this new way of working are interesting, challenging and exciting. What responsibilities do investors have to secure worker protections, from remote and work-from-home to the metaverse? Will the redefinition of work reduce global inequality by empowering new labour segments, or exacerbate it due to telecommunications disparities? Will virtual workplaces solve the global wealth gap?[9]

LIVING WELL AT WORK

Another key question for CO-working, which I posed as a speaker to the 4,000 delegates attending the 2022 Future Investment Initiative conference in Riyadh, is not how do we work well from home but how do we live well at work? Work has become integrated into not only a physical place at home, or at the workplace, but how we live in both these locations. The key question is not 'Where is work?' My grandson will ask his father: 'What did Grandpa mean when he said he was going to work?' You don't go to work. Going to work is now quite the Boomer idea.

The key question is: what is work? Because that itself is changing under the influence of a generation that is trying, far more, to integrate the work they are doing with the lives they are leading. Flexible working is now a right. But this hot-desking, flexible environment has led to a situation of isolation and de-personalization – as we have discussed before, the antithesis of CO. The office of the future is going to be reconfigured increasingly for a generation. Particularly those in the creative industries.

The office will become what I am calling Creative Clusters. A Creative Cluster is not necessarily a workplace, but a pub or a coffee shop where people can gather together in their own fields. Perhaps not regularly, but set up from time to time. Because we have to recognize that you can't escape people. Those that pestered and annoyed you when you sat next to them can still do so online. We cannot avoid social contact. But we need to configure the ways in which a generation will wish to exercise its social connection. Because its members won't necessarily want to do so in a physical place that they go to and return from in a fixed time. This model will be adapted to suit not only the creative industries, corporate workspaces will also be reconfigured to reflect this sense of smaller communities working together in an environment that will reinforce a sense of belonging and CO-working in uplifting curated spaces.

If you ask my generation, 'when is the close of business?' we would probably say five or six o'clock. If you ask a Zennial, it might be midnight. And the start of the day is not at some fixed time: eight or nine o'clock. The start of the day is when the creative juices start working. So, while the workplace is changing rapidly and the need for physical bricks-and-mortar offices is diminishing, there will always remain a significant need to ensure we know how to work with people.

And from a Zennial point of view, this is perhaps more important than ever. Because we cannot simply go to a physical place, or indeed a virtual place, and forget the emotional baggage that all of us have. Zennials may be accused of oversharing, but they are more able to express emotional needs than the generations that came before. And therefore you have to deal with the issue not of where you work, or what your work is, but who you are when you work. KNOWING YOUR WHO is very important when it comes to real CO-working. This is a lesson to be taught by Zennials to Boomers. Because if colleagues have an emotional connection they are much more likely to be able to work better together. The image of worker drones in their cubicles – together but separated – wasting their lives away in the service of the 'man', is not the image of the future Zennials want. This is not the CO workplace. The CO workplace is where true collaboration occurs, where co-workers understand each other on a practical and emotional level. And the trend of productivity is now being reinforced by this Zennial cohort who see greater productivity and a fuller work–life balance as a new liberation from the desk-bound demands of a previous generation. There are some simple tools that can help this environment be realized no matter the make-up of an institution.

I was prompted in this thought by my 25-year-old personal trainer who puts me through my gym routines. He has a very successful father with whom he has a great relationship. When I enquired what the nature of this relationship was, he gave me a quick and forthright answer: 'If I combine my outlook on life and his, we have the perfect combination for doing life. I learn from his experience and skill in business and in return I try to encourage him to develop a great emotional intelligence and empathy with the people he meets.'

One of the noticeable and puzzling features of the Zennial generation is the ability to hold contradictory, often opposing, moral views at the same time and to feel no lack of comfort in expressing these views. Frequently these are dismissed by an older generation as either purely inconsistent or a further example of wanting to have the cake and to eat it. The generational malaise: the inability to commit to a particular view and to hold this consistently. There is clearly an element of truth in this criticism and, again, it is good for the Boomer generation to hold a mirror to this feature of Zennial life.

However, there is a deeper reason as to why Zennials can entertain quite opposing opinions, at times reacting with rage and intensity in a reactionary and conservative way and at the very same time mockingly opposed to these feelings. I believe it occurs as a result of the identity crisis that has hit the generation. The struggle to find a true persona in a complex and conflicted world and to live it out when cancel culture could penalize one or the other strand. This fluidity of identity

179

is reflected in the ambiguity and fluidity of the views that are expressed. This is not an excuse but an explanation. But it should not go unchallenged as this confusion has serious consequences both for the working life and the mental resilience and social interactions of the generation. Wavering indecision is a deterrent to productive activity at work and needs to be called out as such without fear of misunderstanding.

HOW TO DISAGREE WELL

For five years, I chaired The Reconciling Leaders Network for Justin Welby, the Archbishop of Canterbury, the head of the Anglican Church worldwide. The purpose of the initiative was to develop practical tools to help people, wherever they are, understand the importance of learning to disagree well. This is incredibly fertile CO ground because, as we have discussed previously, being *unable* to disagree well is what has led to so much of the disconnection in our world. And being able to disagree well is a crucially important part of building the CO workplace, because it allows for collaboration and learning at every level.

The three key messages of the initiative were as follows[10]:

- Be Curious: listen to others' stories and see the world through their eyes.
- Be Present: show up and stick around, learn to encounter others with authenticity.
- Reimagine: find hope and opportunity in the places where we long to see change.

These are tenets that should be adopted in every workplace that is attempting to bring people of different ages, backgrounds, ideas, ideals and creeds together in order for them to work effectively – a true CO workplace. As Archbishop Justin Welby has said: 'Reconciliation is not the ending of all difference, but the transformation of how we deal with difference.' We need to transform how we deal with difference. That is fundamental to creating a CO world. And fundamental to the way we navigate towards true CO-working.

You may be thinking that practical advice from the Archbishop of Canterbury is not necessarily of the utmost relevance when we're discussing how to overcome obstacles that threaten the foundations of capitalism. However, this is the type of wisdom that will be necessary if we're to advance CO and, in fact, it is crucial that we look outside of the corporate or business world when it comes to redefining capitalism for the future. That's kind of the point. It was being too inward looking and individualistic in the first place that got us into trouble.

But if you're still unconvinced, I'd like to draw now upon advice from a perhaps more familiar outlet, the *Harvard Business Review*. In 2021, Kevin Sharer, former CEO and chairman of Amgen, the world's largest biotechnology company, published an article about listening better – as indicated above, a key principle to building a CO-working world.

In it, he revealed that, when a crisis hit Amgen during his time as CEO, forcing 14 per cent of its staff to be cut, he initially 'angrily blamed others for the debacle'. But he came to realize that he had, in fact, mishandled the crisis, 'in large part because he was a horrible listener'.[11]

He resolved to do better, and Sharer's recommendations about how to improve as a listener in the workplace – 'instead of thinking of eight things at once when he was meeting with somebody, he would be present' – are incredibly practical for how to build a CO-working environment. The article itself is aimed, in the main, at senior executives who 'can become insulated from early signs of danger and opportunity' specifically because of their seniority. Subordinates are wary of giving bad news to them, or they become too busy to notice vital warning signs. As such, this advice might seem like it is only relevant for Boomers, who are currently likely to be in more senior roles than Zennials.

But I don't believe that to be the case. What Sharer and his co-author Adam Bryant describe is an ideal of a CO-working system. They encourage the creation of a 'listening ecosystem', an environment in which listening is undertaken without distraction or judgement. No matter what the environment is, even outside of work, this kind of thinking aligns with CO principles, and the move from *me* to *we*.

Sharer and Bryant conclude their piece with seven steps that can be taken to learn to listen more effectively:

- Protect against blind spots. Which means ensuring every member of a team ensures every other member, including and perhaps most importantly anyone senior, is kept informed.
- De-emphasize hierarchy. This is specifically about ensuring employees aren't intimidated by titles or rank, meaning there is never a block to communication.
- Give permission to share bad news. Basically, always provide the whole picture and ensure that nothing is held back.
- Create an early-warning system. Anand Chandrasekher, CEO of Aira Technologies, has a simple one: if you have bad news, text me; if you have good news, share it with me in person.
- To encourage problem-solving, acknowledge progress. Make it easier for people to talk positively about a problem by illustrating that problems are there to be solved.

- Listen without judgement or an agenda. Don't just be waiting for your moment to speak; learn to listen and respond directly.
- Actively seek input. Perhaps the most important point for every CO worker to remember, because this is where collaboration flourishes.

As I said previously, there is no way to escape people, even in a new workplace that may be virtual or significantly different to what they are now. Disagreements, arguments, anger abound in every place where human beings have to work together. Tensions rise, colleagues get hurt. And that is true whether we're working cheek by jowl or screen to screen. But these tensions can be alleviated in a CO-working environment. You may sometimes feel that you want to escape the people you work with, but the truth is, as ever, that we gain more from working together than working alone. In a CO-working world where everyone listens actively and collaborates effectively, working alone will be seen as the raw deal.

UNDERSTANDING WHY WE WORK DIFFERENTLY

Even in a CO-working world where we are all active listeners and collaborators, there are still going to remain key sticking points, especially intergenerationally, because we work differently. And why do we work differently? Because there is a distinct difference in the *ways* we learned to work when we were at school, being educated. That is not to be as basic as to say that we were taught different things; of course curriculums change over time. But the methodology and environments in which we were educated were different. And it means that the way we learn is different.

Us Boomers were taught a lot of learning by rote. Times tables drills in maths. Reeling off dates in history. That kind of thing. It was linear learning. A led to B led to C. You might call it book-learning. Reading a book from cover to cover was the way to succeed. The teacher stood at the front of the class and provided a lecture. You took down notes. Interactivity was not necessarily prevalent. Teaching 'tech' probably began and ended at the overhead projector.

The school and teaching environment was different too. Not only was the type of technology on offer to assist with learning a world away from what it is now; the relationship between student and teacher was as well. And more of the teachers were likely to have been men. In the US, for example, men made up most of the high-school teaching force until the late 1970s.[12] In the UK at the start of the current decade, over 75 per cent of teachers were women.[13]

Communication between teachers and students went one way when I was at school. And, most obviously, punishments for infractions often had a physical element to them. Indeed, corporal punishment was only prohibited in all state-supported education in the UK in 1986. That ban was not extended to cover private schools in England and Wales until 1998, Scotland in 2000, and Northern Ireland in 2003.

That is a learning environment completely alien to the Zennial. Not least because, as I have already touched upon, hardly any effort is needed today to *find* the information you might require for a particular subject. Your phone or laptop provides all the answers you could possibly need or want. Indeed, information is arguably *too* prevalent. There are *too* many answers out there. This surfeit of information has led a generation to have too much to live with and too little to live for.

Compared to Boomers, Zennials have been taught in what might be termed a significantly more child-friendly environment, technically more constructivist. Constructivism as a theory of education puts emphasis on the engagement of the learner. It posits that individuals or learners do not acquire knowledge and understanding by passively perceiving it within a direct process of knowledge transmission – i.e. by having a teacher drone on at them. Rather, they construct new understandings and knowledge through experience and social discourse – CO-construct, if you will – integrating new information with what they already know.[14] That theory has had a huge impact on the way teaching has developed and reflects the way that Zennials will have experienced education. A school lesson in which a teacher merely stands at the front of the class and reads aloud from a book, or demands the communal recital of the 14 common French verbs that take *être* rather than *avoir*, is unlikely to be seen as acceptable in the twenty-first century. Zennials find it more productive to learn from other people than from a book or a course.

The flexibility accommodated within the learning environment of the Zennial is a world away from the didacticism my generation experienced, when there was only one answer: the teacher's. And there was little way of contradicting that.

It is likely that most would agree that the way in which both school and university students are taught now is an improvement on how it was 50–60 years ago. Engaging students naturally seems like a more productive way of teaching them rather than just demanding that they learn a set of specific facts. But that does not mean you can undo the way in which entire generations were taught, and still like to be taught. Just because teaching practices have changed over time does not mean that someone who was taught to learn in one way will necessarily be able to learn in the new way.

CO-WORKING TOGETHER

This throws up some interesting implications for CO and for how to construct a way to work together intergenerationally when we are trying to reach a common aim. As ever, it requires understanding on both sides.

The most obvious environment in which Zennials and Boomers come into conflict in terms of their educational styles is in educational institutions and, indeed, in the workplace. At a university, say, in 2022, most of the students will be Gen Z with a few flagging Millennials still knocking around, while plenty of the senior faculty will be Boomers. In the workplace, as already discussed, Boomers dominate the senior roles, but Zennials are starting to predominate in terms of pure numbers. These environments are going to be influenced by the different learning styles of the people working in them.

So how do the two separate groups tend to work in the twenty-first century?

Well, as a result of their education, Boomers tend to lean more towards a problem-solver style, while Zennials will have a tendency to lean towards a solution-finder style. 'Baby Boomers thrive on concrete information and structure while Millennials strive for more hands-on and less structured approaches.'[15]

Throughout the business world the way of learning has changed as a result. CO-learning from in-house, experienced colleagues in learning communities throughout the organization is a distinct preference compared to the outsourced model to external tutorials. In this way, corporate values are transmitted but also practical skills are transferred through learning from in-house practitioners without a need for a physical meeting or external classes.

This is a conflict that we have already seen when looking at leadership. And the solutions are the same. The practicalities of how we work together are not difficult. They just need to be understood by both sides. Once again, communication is key to that understanding or else we will remain entrenched in the belief that our own position is best and any alternative method is deeply flawed.

Particularly for the Zennial it is important to appreciate that Boomers were taught in *very* different ways. School and university are the most formative years of our lives and, even when it may have been a long time since we attended them, it is difficult to change the habit of a lifetime. Especially when we have not seen any major problems in the way we have learned. They have served us well up to this point and is it not concrete information that we need in this day and age of fake news and changeable facts?

The actual differences that exist between Boomers and Zennials as a consequence of the way we were taught are fairly straightforward. They boil down to basic things, such as Boomers not liking to be micromanaged, something that a Zennial may simply perceive as collaboration.

It is also necessary to always keep in mind that the value systems between generations will be different. To, however briefly, bring in an undiscussed cohort thus far, Generation X (birth years 1965 to 1980): one of their defining characteristics is a fierce independence, a near pathological need to do things on their own.[16] As a result, they're best left to get on with things.

But this is not true of Boomers and Zennials, who do have a link between them because so many of the latter are sons and daughters of the former. So there is a natural inclination for us to work together. The conflicts between these two groups arise from their close connection, and that is a connection that can be used towards creating a CO world.

It is not possible to change people's life experiences. As we have discussed, the environments in which Boomers and Zennials were forged were very different. So different that they have resulted in two cohorts that have contrasting priorities and methods. But the way to react to that with a CO attitude is to turn it into a strength.

I return, once again, to the combining of the Boomer's hindsight and the Zennial's insight. The two are not incompatible. A knowledgeable Boomer may find themselves frustrated by a Zennial's lack of experience or their need to be provided with specific, detailed instructions. But that is merely them being a result of the environment in which they were taught, which included both incredibly hands-on teachers and helicopter parents. That does not mean they have nothing to offer. Indeed, it is an invitation to work together with them. And to learn from each other.

We have already discussed the need to break out of the silos in which we exist separately. These silos have been formed as much by the difference in our educational upbringings and learning styles as by our relationships with technology. The way we break out of these and practise CO effectively is by understanding that what we can learn from each other and achieve together is of much greater benefit than what we can achieve if we remain separated. What we will discuss in the next chapter further emphasizes the need to understand this.

9

CO-COMPASSION

Compassion is the heart behind the Zennial approach to change. This has major consequences for capitalism as we know it. Because Zennials simply will not allow any system of economic activity to grow that does not have an authentic and expressed compassionate edge, not only in its ESG report, but in its actual day-to-day operations. Impact is what matters most. Impact investing is the comprehensive response of a generation that will not be satisfied by purely financial criteria. We see this everywhere. It manifests itself in obvious ways throughout our everyday lives. When you last visited McDonald's and used their self-service machines, you were almost certainly asked if you wanted to round up your bill to the nearest pound as a donation to charity. This is the impact of Zennial compassion in action. They legitimately care about the world deeply. By this I do not mean that an older generation lacks compassion. But by comparison, Zennials have it much higher up the value curve.

One can argue that this care is expressed in unwise and inflammatory ways, but you could never argue that they don't care. Zennials are deeply motivated by an intrinsic sense of justice, moral imperative, and compassion towards the suffering of the other. Compassion is one of the most fundamental CO principles.

It is often good to fully appreciate the etymological foundations of a word. Compassion literally means to 'co-suffer' or 'suffer with'. '*Passio*' and '*cum*' (respectively meaning 'suffering' and 'with' in Latin) come together in our hybrid language to give us a word that we use to describe sympathy – and even empathy – for another's suffering. This is manifest in our emotional, cognitive and behavioural response: we feel with the suffering, we understand the suffering and we act to alleviate suffering.

THE END OF 'I DIDN'T KNOW'

Today, in the information age, we are exposed to more human suffering than ever before. We know about famine and disease blighting the lives of multitudes. We know about the humanitarian atrocities of Russia's war in Ukraine. We know of church leaders who cover up sexual abuse scandals. We can't use the excuse of 'I didn't know' as our reason for not showing compassion and acting on behalf of others. Beyond simple knowledge – the suffering of the world has come closer to us quite literally. Digital platforms have amplified the voices of the marginalized and have made it possible for all the pain of the world to be expressed more viscerally, and visually, than ever before.

It is one thing to read about a child washed up on the shores of Turkey in a newspaper column. It is a wholly different thing to see it on news reports, websites and the like with your own eyes, over and over again. This, of course, is exactly what happened in 2015 during the Refugee Crisis following the collapse of Syria. While the country was being ravaged by the extremist 'Islamic State', millions of Syrians fled the country and headed west into Europe to try and find refuge. Many attempted to make their way by land while others tried their luck by sea, crossing the Mediterranean to get to safer waters. And one of them was a little boy called Alan Kurdi (two or three years old), who boarded a small inflatable boat on the coast of Turkey en route to Greece along with his family. Less than half an hour after their departure, the boat capsized and Alan Kurdi drowned, along with his mother and brother. His body was discovered early next morning on the beach by the Turkish authorities, where it was photographed.

The world erupted in heartbreak. It is not the first time a child has died as a result of war; countless numbers have been the awful collateral damage of conflict and political violence. Neither is it the first time suffering has been captured on camera. (Indeed, photography has been one of the most powerful mediums of the last hundred years in exposing the human reality of global suffering). But what made Alan Kurdi different, and indeed George Floyd a few years later, is that the channels of dissemination were instant, infinite and interactive. It was not simply readers of *National Geographic* or the *Financial Times* who could see the images or videos and feel a private reaction of disgust and compassion. Everyone could see it, all the time, and could see the reactions of everyone else while they saw it too.

A picture is worth a thousand words as they say. I wonder how much a 4K video is worth? Connection and all the technological marvels it brings with it makes it impossible for us to feign ignorance – no longer can we say: 'I just didn't know.' That means that corporations also cannot say: 'We didn't know.'

Corporations like Facebook, Instagram and YouTube, which are now the air we breathe. They are the streets and forums that we inhabit and where we engage in discourse, and during those weeks following the death of Alan Kurdi, it was as if this child's body was plastered on every billboard, street corner and shop window. You could not escape confronting him face to face. You could not escape the sheer absurdity, outrage and suffering. I know many people who wept at the sight of it. When was the last time you wept for the death of a nameless child thousands of miles away, from a family and a war that has nothing to do with you?

Global suffering is now exposed to us as never before and we can all see it. Indeed, we all have to see it. It's inescapable. And, perhaps reassuringly, it breeds compassion in most. But the way that manifests itself can be different between Zennials and Boomers. This is because many Zennials are forming (or have formed) their morality in this world of bombardment. The same was not true for my generation, who could, in theory, turn a blind eye through lack of the immediacy of knowledge. Or, at least, were not exposed to suffering and injustice in the same visible, continuous and pervasive way Zennials are today. This often leads to misunderstandings between the two generations. On the one hand, there is a weaponization of the word 'woke' and accusations of tokenism against Zennials. On the other, indictments of my generation for being out of touch and/or callous. It is essential that this compassion split is repaired. And I believe there is a solution.

EMBRACING CO-SPIRITUALITY

One of the more enjoyable activities in preparing for my daughter's wedding was the tasting of the cocktails that we would be serving. An expert mixologist, Dan, was on hand to concoct a range of delicious nectars for us to choose from. I asked him what he was trying to achieve in mixing the various flavourings, alcohol, fruits and mixers. He replied that he drew from a wide range of tastes – the bitter, the sweet, the rough, the smooth, the fresh, the preserved – to create a drink that might satisfy the quest for a perfect cocktail. 'Dan, have you ever created a cocktail that fully satisfies?' I asked. 'No,' he replied, 'but that's what life is about. Searching to find the perfect mix of ingredients that will satisfy.' It will not surprise you to learn that Dan is a Zennial. Nor is it unusual to find the cocktail mixologist's quest reflected in the Zennial search for meaning and a true sustaining spirituality in different streams of spiritual experience. Institutional religion is out. We pick and we mix. Spirituality is in. This is the cry. And cry it is, as there remains a desperate and unfulfilled search for purpose and meaning.

A previous generation left a complete vacuum in its scepticism towards the non-material aspects of life. We are not living in a more secular society but in one in which spirituality is growing. It is no longer expressed in and through formal religion, though. As *The Times*' James Marriott has suggested: 'The spiritual need is there; indeed, it is probably more vividly felt by my bewildered, property-less, astrologizing generation than it ever was by the easygoing nihilists of Gen X. Christianity's problem, I think, is that it is no longer aspirational. This may seem a shallow and unspiritual analysis of faith but it is the truth. To succeed, a religion must be socially as well as doctrinally compelling.'[1]

The institutional church will need to take seriously the growing desire of a generation to live an integrated life and to find a space for faith, meaning and fulfilment at work in worship and in the day-to-day activities of the world if it is to engage with a generation that has lost confidence in the institution.

Here, a previous generation nurtured in a dismissive attitude to religion can help to shape a CO-spirituality, learning from a new generation to take spirituality seriously, and adding a critical eye to rein in some of the wilder corrosive excesses of the internet age.

To reflect this growing trend towards spirituality, the BBC has run a Radio 4 series called *The New Gurus*. Such is the proliferation of new gurus through the internet that the series claims a revolution as great as the Protestant Reformation is emerging. There are literally hundreds of thousands of these self-appointed spiritual guides teaching meditation, spirituality and enlightenment. The trademark of the guru, in essence their special sauce, is that they have a secret wisdom that the disciple doesn't have and that they believe disciples should have. Their trade is the giving of advice. Of course not all of it is helpful. The results of an alcohol mixologist's efforts may be intoxicating, but the outpourings of a spiritual mixologist can be dangerously toxic, affecting people's mental state, and their ability to work effectively and to engage in productive economic activity. Naturally there are positive sides. A well-adjusted, integrated and spiritually attuned executive will be more productive in a workplace that values emotional intelligence – compassion – as well as financial calculus.

Russell Brand is a modern example of a guru. The English comedian has turned away from his previous life as a self-proclaimed hellraiser and now preaches to some six million disciples, 'awakening' them through meditation, spirituality and 'advanced gnostic enlightenment'. No longer a stand-up comic, he concentrates his work on leading this voyage of truth and infecting his followers with a religious zeal and frisson of excitement at the forbidden knowledge they are imbibing. He is an example of the way in which empowering technology has enabled a generation not only to become more effective in the workplace but to stream meditation and spiritual apps in their desperate search for a leader or guru to help them navigate the complexities of the financial and working environment and the significant and rapid changes in the workplace, technology and relationships.

In this respect, the iPhone has become the extraordinary empowerment that Steve Jobs always intended it to be. It was never meant simply to be an effective piece of kit; rather, from its inception, it represented a direct challenge to the established order in every sphere of life: a message that resonates effectively with the Zennial generation. But a note of caution has to be sounded. Although the iPhone has empowered Zennials, the mental consequences of confusion are incalculable and a warning sign hangs over those of them who participate in the global financial market. Clearly the search for meaning and purpose in life is not confined to the current generation, but never before have there been so many effective ways for charlatans and others to traduce such a wide group of needy people with, at times questionable, spiritual activity.

This is not to discount the huge value of apps such as Calm and Headspace, which offer genuine meditation to very stressed people at work. I have the privilege of chairing a startup wellbeing app called Glorify, founded by my son. I like to think this is a good practical example of the Boomer and the Zennial combining insight and hindsight. Glorify is a distinctively Christian app aimed at strengthening every Christian every day in the effort to live at peace in a challenging and often hostile world.

Self-realization, which is the thread that runs through the quest for a guru to add a spiritual dimension to life, needs to be tempered by the experience of an older generation who, although they have turned from established religion, nonetheless understand the depth of human consciousness and, above all, the dangers of exclusive introspection. The same is true when it comes to compassion and how to act on the compassion overload that is prompted daily as we read the news and check our social media.

The market economy has clearly benefited from the growth of impact and values-based investing, in great part fuelled by a compassionate world view. So ethical investing, green bonds, water and climate themes have emerged into the mainstream of the financial economy. In a previous generation these values were expressed differently and at the margin largely through charitable foundations. A new generation of investment professionals and steadily capitalized Zennial investors are offered these investments without suffering a reduction in financial returns. Similarly, new pools of long-term infrastructure capital are drawing investment into the developing world to fund life-enhancing projects such as in sanitation, housing, climate protection and biodiversity while still being compensated adequately for these risks.

ESSENTIAL CO-LIVING

In the 1960s, the French-Lithuanian philosopher Emmanuel Lévinas wrote about the importance of the 'Other', specifically, the 'face of the other'. In his 1974 book *Otherwise than Being*, Lévinas wrote: 'A face is a trace of itself, given over to my responsibility, but to which I am wanting and faulty. It is as though I were responsible for his mortality, and guilty for surviving.'

In other words, something special happens when you encounter another person. The recognition of the 'other' – a human being like me who acts like me, and appears to be the master of their conscious life. When we truly internalize the reality of another person, and confront their face, we cannot help but take up moral responsibility for that person's very life. Unlike Descartes' maxim, 'I think therefore I am', in which the only thing anyone can be truly certain of is their own personal existence, Lévinas encourages us to consider that perhaps the most important thing we have to be truly certain of is that the Other exists – that people around you exist as much as you do.

Lévinas's understanding of the impact of the face of the 'other' can be applied to the impact of social media in informing the Zennial sense of moral responsibility and compassion for those they have never met, and also to the imperative requirement to translate this into the *modus operandi* of the businesses they work in. The moral 'emotion gap' that usually exists between those who have never met (meaning that our sense of moral responsibility is most keenly felt for those closest to us) seems to be removed by the instant connection social media creates. No more out of sight, out of mind. If proximity is no longer physical, what happens to morality? Social media means we are constantly in the face of the other. Does the face of the other then need to be redefined? Who is my neighbour?

Not only that, we have been reassessing another fundamental assumption in Descartes' assertion – that human beings are primarily 'thinking things' and that we are motivated by rational reason. When we encounter the other, there is of course a meeting of minds, but there is also the meeting of heart, and flesh 'n' bone, and souls. For close to 500 years, the dominant view of what makes humans unique was our capacity to reason. The now ubiquitous phrase 'I think therefore I am' perfectly encapsulates this view. What makes us fundamentally human creatures is our ability to 'think' – our ability to reason and come to rational conclusions. We are brains on sticks – if our brains were removed from our body and stored in a tank, that would be enough to constitute a sense of 'myself' – I am still in that tank. This model was foundational to the very establishment of the free market. The global economy will flourish so long as people are making rational decisions. This, however, has been well and truly debunked. Perhaps it would be more accurate to say we are hearts on sticks. If we all make decisions with our hearts, not our heads – and that seems to be particularly true for Zennials – then what will be the impact on the global market economy?

THE RATIONALITY MYTH

A mythical creature exists in the realm of economics: the 'Homo economicus'. *Homo economicus* is the rational agent of classical economics, a term coined by the political economist C. S. Devas. His tools are facts, numbers, research, quantitative analysis, indices and indicators. He is rational and utilitarian, a calculating machine on legs. *Homo economicus* is a 'dollar-hunting animal' and will always seek to reap the greatest amount of benefit for the least amount of cost. But this creature does not exist. Ever since episodes like tulip mania, the South Sea Bubble or the tech bubble, it has been painfully obvious that people don't always act rationally. You don't have to look beyond your own home to know this is true. We are emotional creatures driven by deep feelings and our gut. We don't calculate whether to go in for that kiss, or whether or not we take a swipe at our sibling despite the resulting terrible wrath of our parents.

Yet rational choice theory, which states that people will elect to maximize personal advantage if given a free and informed choice, was the basis on which all of us in the financial world worked. This, in turn, was the foundation of the 'efficient market hypothesis', which states that the market price for an asset is the best possible predictor of its price in the future, because all information is distilled into that price.

Essentially, it was the idea that the free market was the perfect mirror to collective rational thinking working well – having millions of people committing their rationality to a global problem will surely provide the most accurate results. It was this rational flaw – this misunderstanding of human identity – that drove the madness of the Global Financial Crisis. There was no need to ask deeper questions about whether rational choice theory was right morally, still less whether it corresponded to reality. People were rational.

Information was available. Calculations were made. Prices reflected this. And the system worked. End of story.

The sad fact, we now know, is that it was not the end of the story. The view of selfhood that animated this model was quite simply wrong. Most obviously, we are not always rational. Indeed, anyone who thinks that humans are naturally and always rational creatures hasn't spent much time with them. Greed overtook performance, individuals went before communities, the short term usurped the long term, the distinction between debt and equity blurred. Banks created credit *ex nihilo*, without calculating the costs to back it up. Institutions believed they could conjure up hundreds of billions of dollars in credit and not take responsibility. Banks are creators of credit, albeit in regulated circumstances, but were not prepared to take on the responsibilities of the creator for their actions.

Governments and individuals also borrowed heavily and did not always spend wisely. In the UK, a policy of increasing public spending with an eye to electoral advantage was financed by running up the government's deficit when the economy was relatively strong. The structural deficit – the gap between government spending and revenues that is considered normal at a given point in the economic cycle – could have been reduced while tax revenues were plentiful. Except that governments did not save for a rainy day. Even a rationally thinking child will know that saving for a rainy day is a good thing to do. Maybe we should have put them in charge?

The result is the revelation – at least it has come as a revelation to some – that the rational self that had underpinned so much of our thinking and activity is illusory. Or, at the very least, wildly inadequate. All of us at some time or other misperceive risk, being unable to calculate the true extent of the chances we take. All of us have a tendency to favour evidence that confirms our existing biases. All of us have a tendency to go with the crowd, and are yet capable of deluding ourselves that our decision is one of courageous autonomy. Our behaviour betrays our belief that we are really that rational.

The world we have inherited has been modelled on these principles. Indeed, we are still largely trapped within the language of the Enlightenment. We tend to view reason, logic, facts and material goods as the defining principles of our lives. The soulful, the spiritual, the numinous, the non-material – these have become alien words in our culture. Words that should be treated with suspicion and disdain; words that no commentator or academic would entertain seriously.

Increasingly we are realizing that our perception of ourselves is a myth. But we still haven't acknowledged the full scale of the problem. The rational Enlightenment citizen is the foundation of our political and economic system. It is the basis on which our institutions and model of the markets and government is run. For the last 300 years – Modernity 1.0 – we have embraced a one-dimensional view of the world that, again and again, has led to unmitigated disaster. We have embraced a radically individualistic, over-rational concept of 'The Self'. This is a false embrace. There is more than this single dimension. And Zennials are seeing this, because they have been exposed to the flaws in the system. T. S. Eliot wrote that 'Last year's words belong to last year's language, and next year's words await another voice.' That new voice is the Zennial one.

THE IMPORTANCE OF NON-ECONOMIC MOTIVATIONS

Fortunately, this is becoming common knowledge in the economic community. After the Global Financial Crisis, economists George Akerlof and Robert J. Shiller published a book called *Animal Spirits: How Human Psychology Drives the Economy, and Why It Matters for Global Capitalism.* They argued just this: that many of the forces that drive our behaviour and actions are not primarily rational, but deeply seeded in our emotions and passions. They write:

> The thought experiment of Adam Smith correctly takes into account the fact that people rationally pursue their economic interests. Of course they do. But this thought experiment fails to take into account the extent to which people are also guided by non-economic motivations. And it fails to take into account the extent to which they are irrational or misguided. It ignores the animal spirits.

These 'non-economic motivations' and the irrational 'animal spirit' are vital to take into account as we move forwards into the future, into the Zennial age. They are not failures of humankind, but the things that make us truly human. These are our multitudes. And they must be factored into our new capitalism.

We are not simply hunter-gatherers who mechanically look to maximize our storehouses and efficiency. We are creatures who are driven by all the heights and depths of human emotion – love and hatred, despair and hope, greed and generosity – to act in ways that feel completely unpredictable and irrational. Zennials understand this.

Outside of economists, philosophers and sociologists have also caught wind of this truth. James K. A. Smith, the philosopher, had a similar recognition that we have been defining the essence of the human person as a *res cogitans* – 'a thinking thing'. 'In other words,' he writes, 'we imagine human beings as giant bobblehead dolls: with humongous heads and itty-bitty, unimportant bodies.'

Smith has argued since the early 2000s that this is a fundamentally flawed vision of what it means to be a human person. In almost all that we do, we are not animated by what we rationally think; rather we are animated by deep values and loves, and our vision of the good life. Humans are fundamentally 'liturgical'; our actions are determined by what we hold to be the thing of ultimate value – i.e. what we worship – the thing that 'captures our loves and longings'. The heart takes the driving seat in Smith's analysis. If you want to find out what a person truly believes in, don't listen to what they say, look at what they do, for that will reveal the truth about their humanity. Being human is so much more than being a brain.

In a similar vein, political scientist Jonathan Haidt argues that we are first and foremost intuitive beings before we are rational ones. We make moral judgements in a flash, and reasoning comes later. And isn't that so true? First impressions matter hugely when, rationally, they shouldn't. Our intellect is a servant to the far more visceral part of our humanity – our emotions and passions. Reason alone isn't the thing that tells us that genocides are bad.

Even in the advertising world, we have recognized that the way to affect behaviour and purchasing habits is not through rational arguments. TV adverts used to tell you five facts about such and such a product and try to convince you that it is the rational one to buy.

In *Thinking, Fast and Slow*, perhaps one of the most important books to have been published in behavioural science, author Daniel Kahneman observes that the human brain works in two 'systems': System 1 and System 2. These two systems work together to produce our thoughts and behaviour. System 1 is the part of our brain that is emotional and instinctive, and System 2 is deliberative and logical. Both are important to engage with when it comes to advertising and persuasion, but System 1 has a disproportionately more significant impact on getting people to act and change their behaviour. If you want someone to choose your shop over another, you don't tell them the ten ways in which your shop is better; rather, you appeal to something deeper.

A prime example of this is the John Lewis Christmas advert. For readers not living in the UK, John Lewis is a UK department store that has become famous for its beautiful and emotionally resonant Christmas adverts – some would say saccharine, but they're Christmas adverts, after all.

These ads have become a tradition, and throughout the autumn, anticipation mounts as to what John Lewis will pull out of the bag. One year, it was a heart-warming story of a child waiting, we assumed, to *receive* all his Christmas presents, only for the reveal to show that the child was actually excited to *give* his gifts; another year, it was the story of a little boy and a pet penguin learning to love one another. They have been the most effective advertising in John Lewis's history.

Why are they so effective? Because they appeal to the heart and associate John Lewis with the best of the warm fuzzies you get during Christmas time. Before these Christmas offerings, John Lewis adverts were focused on how great their customer service was, this being presented as the most compelling rational reason to shop at John Lewis. Funnily enough, those did not do very well.

Every part of human life and study in the last decades has shown us that we are not primarily rational beings. Whether it's in the field of economics, advertising, theology or neuroscience, we have well and truly undermined this notion that we are simply brains on sticks.

THE ZENNIAL RESPONSE

Zennials are the first generation in a long time to have lived without this assumption baked into their psyche and these notions of what it means to be human. Zennials are quick to recognize that arguments are not simply rational back and forths. Morality is not simply a calculation. Justice is not simply procedural. Zennials validate the emotional realities of their peers in a way that is foreign to Boomers. To suggest that it is 'irrational to feel the way you feel' is perhaps one of the greatest Zennial *faux pas*. The Zennials are the first generation in quite a few to truly go out into the world unfettered by the tyranny of rationality – that the only legitimate way to engage with the world's problems and institutions is with our brains.

I am constantly impressed by the number of considerations some Zennials weigh up when making a decision. Not only are they considering them with their heads, they are also feeling them with their gut. It seems that they carry the weight of the entire world, and the fate of every factory worker and Amazon delivery person, on their shoulders. There is such sincere compassion and care to be found in the hearts of young people today. They truly want to be good people who do good to others. This global, interconnected, collaborative way of seeing the world has significantly impacted on established institutions that traditionally would never have been considered for a moment to be within the realm of compassion or ethics – including the financial world. Even how we measure the success of a nation is moving towards models that include deeply compassionate and ethical dials.

For example, gross domestic product (GDP) was, together with GNP (gross national product), traditionally the measure of economic activity. However, Zennials are searching for new measurements and new ways to measure overall success that will calibrate with new measures of environmental impact, social activity and governance (ESG), and so forth, that are to be included in new national indexes of what counts as 'wealth'. These new indexes now screen out companies that score low on these measures, such as those involved in military arms supply chains, those that have a significantly negative impact on the environment, or those that cause social instability through poor employee-management structures or unfair salaries. For investors, ESG funds are becoming a popular alternative to national index funds. Arguably, this creates a truer measure of national prosperity. Because it doesn't look purely at economics, but establishes a way of measuring, holistically, economic wellness in human (or perhaps that should be non-economic) terms as well.

On a fundamental level, this shift is motivated by compassion. The sense that Zennials have of feeling personally responsible for the future of humanity. This is CO – the expansion of the self to encompass both you and the other. *We* rather than just *me*. The expansion of vision to synthesize and include considerations that in previous generations had no place to be thought of together – like GDP and ESG. The expansion of moral responsibility to suffer with the refugee and their hurting, regardless of distance. The collective moral standards of the Zennials are incredibly high.

WHAT IS CO-COMPASSION?

True compassion – the kind of compassion that will bring about a CO world – is one that requires the most compassion towards your enemies and those you seek retribution against. Anger and rage can stir a revolution, but they will cause schisms in our society in the process.

I imagine if you are reading this, you are a well-informed, globally minded person who has some opinions about the ethical demands on your life, be that about your responsibility concerning the environment, race relations or economic systems. I imagine some of you care very deeply about these topics and will debate into the night with your peers what we as a collective society ought to do and what maxims each citizen ought to follow on any given day.

We should recycle and try to replace as many household items with reusable or zero-waste products as possible. We should be voting not just with our ballots but with our wallets. So on and so forth. These are all good things to be discussing and, to be sure, working out what rules we ought to live by together will be an incredibly important aspect to realizing our CO dream.

Many of these rules are motivated by compassion for the poorest in our world. However, we must be careful to avoid laying too heavy a load on the shoulders of people who lack the resolve or headspace to consider such things deeply. If you are reading this book, it is worthwhile recognizing that you are most likely intellectually privileged above many others you share your life with and this privilege goes a very long way – arguably further than material privilege.

What may seem like obvious maxims and rules for you that you can implement easily into your life may very well be incredibly onerous for another. Perhaps a better way to put this is that we must show compassion towards those who lack the ability to display it as much as we do. It can be easy to feel compassion towards those who can't help themselves but rather harder when it comes to those who can only just about help themselves.

Compassion is a must. It is necessary for CO. And it requires something of us. It requires commitment and resolve to follow through on the initial pangs of pathos so that it crystallizes into will and action. It requires us to consider the 'Other' as truly real and for us to take responsibility for their wellbeing. It requires us to continually soften our hearts to suffering. It requires us to give the benefit of the doubt and be merciful to those who lack compassion.

10

CO-CREATING

In the introduction to this book we established that there is a major, and crucially unstoppable, shift occurring in our society; a shift that could destroy capitalism as we know it if it is not tackled in a considered manner. This shift is one of power, influence and capital moving from one generation to another. From Boomers to Zennials, two groups that, as we have seen, spend a great deal of their time thinking there is more that separates them than unites them. We must rectify this if we are to create a new way of living and a sustainable capitalism that will see us flourish over the coming decades. It is an economic imperative that we do so.

And it is a global imperative. For as we again discussed in the introduction, this shift is occurring worldwide. The changing face of the market economy is reflected in the movement of capital not only from old to young, but also from West to East towards Asia, as well as in the switch from brown to green energy as the world looks to decarbonize, and from men to women as the move towards real gender equality continues apace.

We have analysed the fissures that exist in our society in the 2020s – the intergenerational tensions, the individualistic capitalism, the dangers of technology, and the mutability of truth and facts. And we have established that it is through CO that we might repair these fissures and build a new, stronger capitalism that is more equitable but that still incentivizes innovation and profit rather than slipping into a collectivism that stunts growth and progress. Crucial to achieving this aim is learning how to CO-lead, CO-work and show compassion. The final CO tenet we will look at, and perhaps the most crucial, is learning how to CO-create.

THE NECESSITY OF INNOVATION

Co-creation is already a defined practice in the business world. Indeed, a recent *Forbes* article was headlined: 'Co-Creation: A Powerful Tool For Organizations Looking To Become More Innovative'.[1] The piece was outlining the necessity for businesses to innovate if a recession in the US was to be avoided, and co-creation was recommended as a route to innovation. As defined by Muthu De Silva, Assistant Dean at Birkbeck, University of London, co-creation is 'the process of developing products or services in collaboration with customers or other stakeholders'.[2] The benefits, the piece outlined, are that co-creation allows businesses to better understand the needs and wants of their customers or clients and develop new ideas and solutions accordingly.

Now, we are not looking at the relationship between businesses and clients, nor are we looking at how to develop products. However, we are trying to work out how we can better understand each other's needs and develop new ideas and solutions accordingly. So, if we expand the already extant definition of co-creating to fit our needs, we end up with CO-creating. And CO-creating is a key part of how we go about repairing the fissures that we have discussed thus far and building a new capitalism.

Innovation is essential to the development of CO. Not just innovation of products or thinking, but innovation of the whole system. CO is the shift from the radical individualism of post-war generations to a prioritization of collaboration, compassion, community and collective experience. This is the innovation that is required to facilitate the shift from *me* to *we* while still preserving capitalism in the form we want it. This shift from *me* to *we* involves understanding that what individuals can gain from working together in CO is greater than what they give up in order to participate.

A new capitalism needs to be created to avoid the whole system disappearing forever. This capitalism cannot be created by one individual or one group – Boomers or Zennials can't do it alone. Indeed, any attempt to create and innovate alone in this respect will be doomed to failure, which is where CO-creating comes in. Because, as indicated above, CO-creating takes into account the needs and ideas of all stakeholders. In this situation, that means Zennials and Boomers working together. The insight of the newer generations combining with the hindsight of the older: the only way to avoid either generation's shortcomings from upsetting the whole project. It also means East and West working in collaboration for CO to be globally realized. And it means brown energy collaborating with green energy in order to facilitate the move to net zero.

INDIVIDUALISM AND CO-DESTINY

This is the rejection of individualism that I have talked about so regularly throughout this book. It was radical individualism that destroyed the foundation of trust which led to the 2008 Global Financial Crisis, which in turn played such a major role in the distrust of and acrimony towards their Boomer parents from the soon-to-be empowered Zennials. So this problem must be solved with collaboration. With CO.

CO-creating means that everyone has a stake in what the results are and everyone's input is valued. In our old version of capitalism, which we must now leave in the past, hierarchy was well established. The ideas came from the top and those further down the ladder did the work to put those ideas into action. This is not the way that Zennials want to work any more. Nor is it the most productive way for anyone to work, as it means ignoring ideas that could be beneficial to any organization. It also ignores the wider idea of an organization having a purpose that every member of staff can share in. And purpose is absolutely crucial to the future of capitalism, because purpose is no longer just purely about making money. It is about ensuring that an organization and its employees share the same ethos and values.

There has been plenty of discussion about purpose in recent years, not least in the wake of the pandemic. People, particularly Zennials, no longer want to just work for a pay packet, they want to have a reason to put in the hours. Each individual has a purpose – defined by McKinsey's Naina Dhingra as 'this idea of having a sense of direction, intention, and understanding that the contribution you're making is going somewhere'.[3] And employees want to know that the organization they work for has one too, ideally one that aligns with theirs.

The term I prefer to purpose is CO-destiny. Because an individual's purpose doesn't exist in a vacuum. In order for someone's purpose to be realized they need to be aligned with their colleagues, their bosses and their organization. CO-creating, then, can only come about if everyone shares in CO-destiny, because sharing purpose is the way to ensure that everyone is working towards the same ideas. CO-destiny is the inverse of individualism, which is why it should play a crucial role in our capitalism as we move forward. This is not just about collaboration; it is about sharing a stake, which then means that everyone is implicated in both success and failure and all join in the future trajectory of the organization and the cooperative ventures being created.

ARTIFICIAL INTELLIGENCE AND CO-DESTINY

With the battle for dominance in the space of AI between Microsoft and Google, between ChatGPT and Bing, dominating headlines, a new era is starting which will redefine not only how we work but our future destiny as human participants in the technological universe. This race sparked an open letter from The Future of Life Institute signed by 2,000 luminaries, including the likes of Elon Musk and Steve Wozniak, co-founder of Apple. The letter called for a temporary suspension of AI training until effective ways can be found to assess the very serious threat to human competitive intelligence posed by AI. The letter asks: 'Should we develop non-human minds that might eventually outnumber, outsmart, obsolete and replace us?' This is the central CO-destiny question of our time. Here is an example of an older generation exercising wisdom and restraint in the face of the hurtling speed of the Zennial quest to drive technology into new spaces without regard to the human consequences. Restraint, unfashionable in a Zennial generation seeking to crash headlong into new areas of machine learning, is a vital contribution an older generation can make, as it is together that we must shape the future of humanity.

SHARING RESPONSIBILITY

When we talk about sharing responsibility what we mean more colloquially is: we are all in this together. Zennials are adamant about the need to incorporate this idea into the market economy, and it is already becoming clear that this shared responsibility will be a key tenet of the future of capitalism. Projects like the

B Corp movement, which provides for-profit companies with certification of their social and environmental performance – represent this idea perfectly. B Lab – which awards B Corp status – is a 'nonprofit network transforming the global economy to benefit all people, communities, and the planet'.[4] It provides certification for businesses to mark out companies that are 'leaders in the global movement for an inclusive, equitable, and regenerative economy'. The fact that something like B Lab exists at all is proof of the increasing desire for corporations worldwide to prove that they are taking their social and environmental impact into account when it comes to their business practices. And if companies themselves are not prepared to adapt, they are being forced into it by enthusiastic activists.

A recent example of a major corporation being caught out in its failure to share responsibility was ExxonMobil, the American oil and gas corporation and the sixth largest corporation in the US according to the 2022 Fortune 500.[5] In May 2021, Exxon was forced to install three new directors on their board after a tiny hedge fund called Engine No. 1 succeeded in its bid to force the company's leadership to reckon with the risk of failing to adjust its business strategy to match global efforts to combat climate change. 'Exxon's Board Defeat Signals the Rise of Social-Good Activists' was the headline the *New York Times* ran on the story.[6] Engine No. 1 owned just 0.02 per cent of Exxon's shares, but using that tiny bit of leverage they managed to persuade some of the corporation's larger shareholders – chiefly BlackRock, the Vanguard Group, and State Street – to back their campaign. In response, Exxon expanded its board and added a director with sustainable investing experience.

Engine No. 1's strategy in forcing the change was actually based more on the impact on Exxon's profitability than on its environmental principles, or lack thereof. But, fascinatingly, the origins of the campaign came about at a family dinner. In

2019, the hedge fund's executive chairman Christopher James was challenged by his school-aged sons at the dinner table. How, they asked, could he consider himself an environmentalist if he invested in energy companies.[7] From these family discussions he would eventually be the key catalyst for change at one of the world's biggest energy companies.

This is purpose, or CO-destiny, in action. And the campaign that eventually forced change at Exxon was a prime example of CO creation. It wasn't a one-man campaign. Indeed, James himself could not have achieved it on his own. He needed BlackRock and other institutions to back him, but he also needed his socially conscious young sons to give him the concept in the first place.

THE MOVE TO CO-LEARNING

The above type of compassionate disruption is only going to increase as the number of Zennials in the workforce increases and they move into more and more powerful positions. If ExxonMobil is not immune to it, then companies worldwide need to realize that they must either adapt or die; or indeed be forced to adapt. It is the same for the Boomers who currently hold the positions of power. The numerical advantage Zennials are building will soon be insurmountable, and there is no need to resist when Boomers are a crucial part of the CO-creating process.

At the heart of CO-creating is the need for input from all areas, and that means Boomers advising Zennials, steering them away from mistakes that may have already been made in the past. It means sharing a purpose that is formulated by both groups. And it also means harnessing the expertise of all. The obvious direction in which expertise will flow is from Boomer to Zennial. The older generation have the experience, the wisdom, and they will be able to pass that on in the same way they are passing on capital, power and influence.

However, in the new world of CO-living, CO-creating, CO-working and CO-destiny, it must also be understood that there are ways in which Zennials can support Boomers. This is the all-in-this-together approach. Finding expertise in every area possible and deploying it in the most beneficial way.

An obvious example of this is in the use of tech. Back in 2020, in the midst of the pandemic, a YouGov poll found that productivity was being slowed by tech-illiteracy in senior employees. As reported by Unily, the company that commissioned the poll,[8] 'one in three employees over the age of 40 requested support for simple technology queries at least once a week, with junior employees reporting that lack of tech skills in senior staff consistently disrupts their workflow and slows productivity'.

One of the solutions mooted for this issue was the concept of 'reverse mentoring'. In other words, senior members of staff being trained by junior members of staff. It is obvious where this could have huge potential benefits. In the tech sphere certainly, and in the use of social media in particular, which has such a huge bearing on society in the 2020s. However, despite the obvious potential benefits of such a scheme, 79 per cent of the employees surveyed said they did not have a reverse-mentoring programme in their workplace.

There is a huge opportunity here to facilitate intergenerational reconciliation through learning, or indeed, CO-learning. Because it is in this type of scenario that barriers come down. CO-creating and CO-learning share the advantage of levelling the playing field somewhat between senior and junior figures at an organization, allowing each different cohort to show their value to the other. And this is empowering not just for junior employees, who can prove their skills in a way that might have been impossible a decade or so ago, but also for senior figures, who can break down the barriers that are often put up simply by the nature of their job title.

In the old capitalism, an idea like reverse mentoring would probably have been laughed out of the room. But in a world where Zennials are predominating and there is a less hierarchical structure in place, it is the kind of initiative that could have a huge impact on productivity. Because active, lively, critical CO-learning between Boomers and Zennials is not just about reconciling the two groups with each other; it is the methodology through which organizations can get the best ideas and innovations out of their employees, and in turn the best results.

THE FOUR HORSEMEN OF THE CAPITALIST APOCALYPSE

I was an adviser to Anglo American plc, a mining company that was founded in 1917 by Ernest Oppenheimer. In 1954, Oppenheimer said of the Anglo American Group: 'The aim of this Group is, and will remain, to make profits for our shareholders, but to do so in such a way as to make a real and lasting contribution to the communities in which we operate.'

For its time, that was a prescient and admirable goal. Few would have batted an eyelid had he simply stopped after the word 'shareholders'. Making a lasting contribution to the communities in which we operate is a particularly CO aim, and one that can be realized by every organization if the principles of this book are followed. Indeed, it is the principal aim for Zennials. But that is not to say that they ignore the first part of it. The difference is that a Zennial CEO today would, perhaps, reverse the sentence: 'The aim of this Group is, and will remain, to make a real and lasting contribution to the communities in which we operate, and to do so in such a way as to make profits for our shareholders.'

That is a fairly good summation of how we might navigate the narrow path towards the more inclusive, purposeful capitalism that still incentivizes good business. Namely, by harnessing both the good intentions and insight of Zennials and the hard-earned experience and hindsight of Boomers to create a CO world.

But as I have said over and over, it is a risky and danger-filled path that we are taking, and I'd like to finish this chapter by warning of the four most dangerous pitfalls that face us: the four horsemen of the capitalist apocalypse, if you will. These are individualism, idealism, intransigence and ignorance. At times throughout this book I have touched on all of them. Individualism needs to be left in the past, it has been consigned to history by the 2008 Global Financial Crisis. Idealism needs to be curbed. This is particularly true for Zennials, who need to understand that a dose of reality is necessary every now and then to ensure the pathway is smooth. This can be provided by Boomers. The avoidance of intransigence is a necessity for everyone. Intransigence is what has tribalized us and consigned us to our silos. Many hear but few listen. We need to listen to other views and be prepared to change our own in order to break out of these. And ignorance, a failure to learn from mistakes of the past and present, will trip us up on our way towards the new capitalism.

CO is the antidote to these mistakes. Whether it's CO-leading, CO-working, CO-compassion, CO-creating, CO-destiny or CO-learning, the understanding that we gain more from working together than working apart is what will steer us away from the destruction of capitalism. The move from *me* to *we* is a challenging one, but it is more achievable than we realize. We have the resources, we simply need to bring them together with CO.

CONCLUSION

Former British Prime Minister Winston Churchill once said: The longer you can look back, the farther you can look forward. The next generation have looked at the expressed desire of the post-war generation to build an inclusive community for humanity based on reason, freedom and science. But they have seen it fail.

THE GENERATIONAL STAND-OFF

Divisions at every level of society are growing, not healing. Access to financial advice and markets have shown inequality deepening economic divides. In a crude meme, the 'haves' still have yachts, and the 'have-nots' are slipping into greater relative economic inequality. As a result, the desire for authentic community burns strongly in the next generation's conscience. And with it a growing passion for fairness and justice. This generation will increasingly flex their economic, social, technological and moral muscles to see this come about. It would be a dangerous stand-off between the generations if this division were to persist. Samuel P. Huntington's *Clash of Civilizations* would rapidly give way to the Clash of Generations as the single most important threat to sustainable economic growth.

I believe that this generation will want to advance a cohort of CO not merely on the basis of reason, science and freedom, which the post-Enlightenment has suggested and which has been embraced by a previous generation. Zennials have seen that this framework has not produced the community that they aspire to. What is so significant is that there is a desire to add a spiritual dimension in the search for community. This is a generation that is spiritually intelligent, in contrast to the previous generation, which dismissed even the notion of spirituality as being irrelevant to the life of society and of no consequence to the economy.

For many, the dream of the previous generation to establish a viable community has not had the necessary glue to hold it together. The next generation wishes to shape an entirely integrated worldview that has a different community at its heart. One that would draw together the economic advantages in terms of incentives, creativity and value-added capitalism, but that has a social energy that can only be realized and unleashed in a community. This *socially energized capitalism* could be the very renewal the market economy needs in order to survive.

Zennials see this as the necessary antidote to the fact that there are still wars, deep divisions and societal unrest. Not to mention the macro-level issues such as nuclear threats, and major moral, social and political confusion. The dream of establishing a vibrant community, based upon rationalist assumptions, then, has proven a failure.

CO-destiny is the way to avoid a clash of generations between Boomers and Zennials, through a new coming together in which the future can be shaped. Both want to see the fruit of CO-creation in unity, social justice and racial equality, but have failed to understand the root of disagreement and how to cope with it.

A community cannot simply be built on the basis of a set of common objectives derived mostly from the observable world around us. It needs additional cement to motivate and draw people together. This is a generation that is anticipating a renewed social contract and knows that it will have both the financial capacity and the motivation, power and influence to tackle the root cause of the brokenness and be able to navigate a new community. They see the societies in which they live as not only broken but broke, with levels of sovereign and personal debt never seen before. A debt they know they will have to bear, even as they struggle to find affordable rent, let alone homes to buy, or to ascend the property ladder, while the generation in whose hands the debt grew enjoys the prosperity of asset inflation.

In order to pay off this debt, integrated, socially energized market-led objectives need to be established. Ones in which profit, living with purpose, and common values are not mutually exclusive, but intricately interwoven throughout the fabric of the market economy. As a newscaster recently proclaimed: 'Even if you give up Netflix, you're unlikely to be able to afford a deposit anytime soon.'[1] There is one key statistic that explains why Zennials currently find it so much more difficult to buy a home than it was in previous eras; namely, how fast property prices have increased relative to earnings. The average price of a home in the UK has increased almost twice as much as the wages of the average worker over the past 50 years.

It is the vigilance of the Boomer generation that will become one of the cornerstones in building this renewed capitalism. In the face of what might become a purely ideological onslaught on the market economy, co-opting the experience of the previous generation will ensure that the narrative of a robust market-driven, value-creating economy will not be lost in a meta-narrative of simplistic and unrealistic social objectives.

THE CLASH OF LIFE AND WORK

Several years ago, I wrote a book called *God at Work*. It was a religious book, but its central claim was the need to have a purpose for going to work each day. Statistics show that the average person will spend about 70,000 hours at work over the course of their lifetime. This is a significant part of a person's life journey, and yet many find themselves lacking any real sense of joy and purpose in it.

People feel overwhelmed by the challenges presented at work; many are underwhelmed by its monotony. A large group of people feel underappreciated in their workplaces, and many are experiencing exhaustion because they are overworked. The pressure to conform to the 'hustle and grind' culture places a precedence on boasting about long hours, little holiday time, and 'there's plenty of time to sleep when I die' mantras that can bleed into what we prioritize, and the goals we set and pursue. Finding a sense of meaning in our work is, therefore, an essential element for anyone wishing to experience a fulfilled life, whether that is driven by having a personal faith or not. As the religious tide has ebbed in the West so the need for purpose has become even more acute. However tenuous the definition may be, nobody wants to work in a not-for-purpose organization.

The global pandemic amplified and accelerated the collision of two distinct worlds: the home world of work, and the workplace, bringing to the fore the question: 'What exactly does work mean to me and what role does it have in my life?' Is it simply a way of securing income that facilitates my lifestyle or is it something more purposeful and purpose filled?

An individual's purpose is an overarching sense of what matters in their life. You might like to think about it as a person's 'North Star'. The idea is that each of us can have a sense of direction and intention, and possess an acute awareness that the contribution we are making is going somewhere and leading towards an intended end. We all intuitively know when we are living with purpose, as we wake up each day feeling energized, inspired, motivated and fully alive to face the constant challenges of the world.

A recent study[2] conducted by McKinsey shows that about 70 per cent of people say they define their purpose through work. Millennials, even more so, are likely to see their work as their life calling as they seek to associate with companies that focus on being a force for good. Finding fulfilment at work is essential.

In contrast, we see the growth of the 'quiet quitting' trend discussed in Chapter 1: Zennials whose hearts are not in their work and merely go through the daily motions. It is a mindset whereby doing the bare minimum of what is required is escalating in the workplace. The mind is at work, but the heart has already left. Its consequences are serious as it leads to a disengagement by employees and a decline in motivation and productivity. We must address purpose at work. We must acknowledge that 'work for me' is dead to a Zennial and the cry 'work with me' is the zeitgeist. It is meaning, not only money, driving this growing percentage of the workforce.

The question is who should adapt to who? The Zennial cohort expects work to adapt to their lifestyle and not for them to bend to the lifestyle imposed by work. Although this is a trend, the importance of older and more experienced leaders listening to these desires for greater fulfilment and working together for solutions is vital. This intergenerational grappling is the exciting part in revitalizing a hope-filled CO-destiny of the generations at work.

THE INFINITE GAME

There is another important factor to be addressed in this intergenerational change in the workplace. When I started my career, it had four phases: obtain a degree (full time and no student loans); join a secure professional institution; maybe change jobs a few times but not many; later in life go plural in part-time work and finally end up with a good pension and no mortgage on my home, if not homes.

Hardly any of this applies to the Zennial. There is one lifelong, ill-defined blur, not four phases, as their generation can expect life expectancy to be 85 if not longer. As writer and thought leader Simon Sinek notes: 'This generation is playing an infinite game, where they see no finish line, only an increase in opportunity and experiences. The planning horizon has contracted to that which is the immediate presenting choice.'

Student loans are a burden lasting for decades. Job security has vanished, and Zennials would expect to change employment with high frequency. Owning a home is a global out-of-reach hope. Retirement is seen as a distant and quaint Boomer aspiration and not a reality. Work–life balance is essential to wellbeing and health, so the place of work needs to cater for this, including time off to retrain and upskill, as well as spend time with family. Many workplaces have adapted to this, changing demands to remain competitive in the job market.

What is needed is a renewed robustness and resilience to ensure these demands are catered for by the largely older senior executives without destroying productivity. We, the older cohort, need to show a greater understanding of the destructive power of the 24/7, 'always on' digital links that drive the Zennial. With a generation's office in their pocket, it will become increasingly important to communicate the very real dangers around the possibility of burnout and unsustainable work patterns and rhythms of life. The number of Zennials suffering from mental health issues is an explosive indictment of our times. If my generation can provide supportive help in creating the networks and personal space needed to facilitate the working from home trend and to mitigate the pandemic effect of loneliness, this will be a very effective and powerful tool for the next generation to thrive and flourish.

Through sharing, with hindsight, their mistakes and failures at work and in relationships, Boomers can be an invaluable help to the struggling Zennials as they navigate the frightening speed of change in their patterns and places of work. But it equally requires the Boomers to be attentive to and not dismissive of the insights of the next generation, as the latter try to cope with the demands of an economy that seems to be excluding them from fully enjoying the benefits taken for granted by the previous generation.

This book has reviewed the ways in which CO can help both an older generation and a younger one find meaning and purpose in a rapidly changing, increasingly hostile and very threatening world. At its heart has been the argument that the silos and tribal divisions that divide the generations have added to the anxieties and complexities that both have faced.

While technological advancement has given us the ability to communicate with groups all over the world with immediate speed and accuracy, it has not become the hoped-for bridge-builder between the generations. On the contrary, without bemoaning the development of technology, its very innovation has exposed an even greater chasm.

We have access to spell-check, voice-dictation, AI, auto-suggestion and other linguistic devices that we could never have imagined 30 years ago. We can have every question we need answered within seconds thanks to a Google search bar, not to mention avenues for communication such as e-mail, WhatsApp, text, tweets, and other platforms. We have face recognition, Siri and Alexa, and other audio activation devices. We can record our speech via apps that cater to our diction, intonation and vocal patterns. Keywords on social media have replaced traditional advertising, and the convenience of tweets and blog posts has replaced thoughtful, authentic discussion on nearly every topic.

Technological advances have, in fact, impaired the way we correspond, connect and communicate with each other. Like a flood spilling across a river's banks, technology may cover more surface area than ever before, but it lacks the depth needed to create a current of effective understanding and communication between generations.

The new kids on the block demand change. We read about their activism in the news every day. From Greta Thunberg's climate advocacy, the #NeverAgain Campaign to #BlackLivesMatter, more and more young people around the world are rising together behind a social cause. Well travelled and globally connected, Zennials are very aware that humanity is facing significant global issues and they feel a sense of responsibility to fix what's broken. As they enter and start to dominate the workplace, they will expect to be able to make significant contributions in a short period of time by exploring new ways of thinking, working and addressing problems.

Boomers, however, are seen by this cohort as more resistant to change, with a tendency to rely more on their past experiences, frequently trying to tame Zennials' need for change instead of enabling it. The older generations, on the other hand, often complain about Zennials' lack of maturity, knowledge, discipline, patience and focus, alongside the lack of respect and appreciation they show for those with many more years under their belt.

This results in having different age groups distracted from their work by a seething sense of mutual resentment. Poor communication combined with conflicting expectations can be a source of tension between generations and leads to a series of seemingly insurmountable intergenerational conflicts in the workplace. That hinders not just an employer's ability to retain talent, but the opportunity to leverage on each generation's unique strengths to drive impact and innovation.

Not only has there been a sense of distrust and disenfranchisement between generations, but there has been a distinct decrease in self-belief and self-efficacy. The Boomer generation have begun to doubt the continued contribution it can make to a world that has become almost unrecognizable, as technology has changed the very nature of life and continues to change at an accelerating pace.

As the cultural landscape shifts regularly, Boomers are threatened daily by the confident encroachment of a younger generation, who seem to have the modern world at their fingertips. The latter have very little doubt about the direction they wish to pursue in terms of their anticipation of internet 3.0, their understanding of developments in culture, crypto currencies, the metaverse and every other aspect of social intercourse. They absorb every rapid change in technology without skipping a beat. Digital communities, like those on Discord, are established, with the aim of creating a genuine human community and connection, built on freedom, justice, reason, and a quality of life that embraces the entire human experience, but without a transcendent, non-material dimension.

THE ANXIETY CURE

Most reports, analytics and articles are quick to state that the space previously occupied by the Church is now a place of irrelevance. A secular theology has been formed, and an expressed dogma that is being lived out with profound effects on the capital market but also on this generation's mental health. This new prophetic generation has become the evangelists for a new, integrated, values-driven world that energizes them and brings identifiable social proof that validates their belief systems. This is the underpinning of the new capitalism that is there to avoid the destruction of the whole capitalist ecosystem if the current divisions continue.

Yet underlying this super-confident, connectivity-seeking, competent generation is an unprecedented level of anxiety. The certainties have proved, unsurprisingly, a failure when faced with the moral and ethical issues that have to be grappled and engaged with. When Google can't give you an answer, and Alexa won't give you a response, where do we go for a clear answer?

Through CO-destiny, we can work out a human way to ensure the security of our futures and the vitality of the market economy. This is how the intergenerational divide on purpose can be settled. The hindsight, experience and lessons of the Boomer help to create wisdom, perspective and understanding, enabling the next generation to learn by instruction rather than having to learn through injury. As markets fluctuate, and political unrest ensues, the Boomers can offer invaluable insights to the Zennial regarding how to stay focused and maintain a strong desire to make a difference in an ever-changing world. As ever we learn by what is caught as much as what is taught.

It is quite clear that the survival of the market economy and its ability to deliver sustainable growth through the next generation is significantly dependent on whether there can be harmonious alignment, particularly between the experience of a generation now in command and that of the emerging generation's ability to create a partnership that will avoid the excess of volatility. And this will be accentuated by the measures needed to ensure that the pace of technological change, the economic outlook for the future, and especially the speed and advancement of AI, is not advanced against our common human interests.

While generational differences are often overlooked, buried under the sand, or simply ignored, they will now play a major part in either stagnating progress or catalysing change. Our world is in desperate need of both the experience and knowledge of the older generations, and the energy and social-mindedness of today's youth. And while it's undoubtedly true that Millennials and Gen Z understand what is important to society at large, it is also true that they will need the support of Boomers and Gen X to turn their aspirations into reality.

Zennials can help Boomers get out of their comfort zone and embrace the tools that are going to shape the next several decades – like artificial intelligence and social media. Areas where they, not Boomers, are often the more experienced ones. This is why it is imperative to keep an open dialogue between the two, and to adapt our approach to reflect a humility and willingness to explore unfamiliar ideas and unexplored approaches.

Mutual humility from both sides comes through active and intentional listening. Especially as it pertains to the capital markets. How we listen and respond can avoid catastrophic insensitivity in the workplace. CEOs have been driven out; shareholders have been left disenfranchised. Mutual reciprocity between employer and employee has all but disappeared. No capital market can exist without effective clear and sensitive communication of the company's vision, and mission statement and purposes. This impacts on external factors, such as investors and markets, but also internally, to build effective and productive executives and, above all, encourage clear decision making.

US pastor and author, Rick Warren, wrote a bestselling book *The Purpose Driven Life*. Its opening line is: 'It's not about you'. A truism that is key to the future of the new era. Together, both generations can become purpose partners, and purpose pushers. Enhancing each other's strengths, establishing a greater sense of purpose at work, and expanding their capabilities in ways they could not effectively accomplish with the same degree of efficiency on their own.

This relates not only to the workplace but also to evaluating critical decisions regarding the future of the capitalist ecosystem. The reason this is important is that we are confronting as humankind an entirely new breakthrough as to what reality actually means. This will affect every economic judgement we make in future.

Against the background of quantum computing, artificial intelligence and machine learning the real world is changing before our very eyes. It is vital that the generations cooperate in both analysing and promoting the enormous advantages that come with these new breakthroughs in our understanding of reality, but also to be firm about the ways in which the dangers are to be monitored, explained and regulated.

And in this new paradigm as significant as the Newtonian revolution, we will need to harness the energies and strengths of every participant in the economic development of society. But what will happen if, in a new artificial-intelligence-driven world, this dominant human collaboration moves away from what is central to being peripheral?

LOOKING FOR SPIRITUALITY

In previous generations faith provided clear guardrails and a clarity of guidance in establishing the correct moral choices the capitalist system needed to face, and offered its own assessment as to the correct course of actions in light of what institutions had to face. In many faiths, this is still the case. Muslims, for example, will find it odd that the silos created in the West between religious observance and daily work still persist.

A later generation assumed that reason, the logic of life, would be the determinant of all forms of reality. What could not be rationally known and scientifically verified could not be regarded as real. Religious beliefs were meant not just to be believed but to be lived, to orient behaviour, attitudes and interpersonal actions towards oneself and others in person-defining ways that affect every encounter and dimension of one's social reality. The capitalism of today shapes people in profound ways that rival the influence of religion on them.

Later generations still assumed that reason, logic and data would be the ultimate determinant of all forms of reality and moral reasoning. What could not be known scientifically or verified empirically could not be regarded as valid or reliable. Under the rubric of its robust work ethic, contemporary capitalism singles out individuals in a highly moralizing fashion for either praise or blame and forces them into competitive relationships with one another. Economic success or failure becomes one's individual responsibility. The effect is to reduce a person's identity to one's financial triumphs or defeats. Cast in such intensely individual terms, success or failure becomes a function of competitive struggle; one doesn't succeed or fail along with others but against them.

While this generation is overtly dismissive of any non-material assumptions and individuals or institutions that claim to own the truth, remain steadfast to their convictions, and leave no room for compromise to establish common ground, we must ask the question: is this purely scientific and rational approach to life working?

Everywhere I go, I see there is a deep search within this generation to find and discover an authentic spirituality that they can integrate and immediately apply to every aspect of their life. From the workplace, through worship, to everyday engagement and interactions in the world. A generation that intuitively emphasizes and embodies values that transcend everyday norms and embodies empathy for others that desperately seeks to express itself.

In his seminal work *God is Back*, John Micklethwait, a former editor of the *Economist*, opened: 'As the world becomes more modern it is not becoming more secular. Instead, on the street and in the corridors of power, religion is surging.' As *God is Back* shows, for better or worse, faith is on the increase.

This, for many, is still a steep hill to climb. They have entered a world where the previous generation remains sceptical and suspicious about sharing personal beliefs and deep emotional needs. Let alone openly exposing one's vulnerabilities. Emotional intelligence is still seen as an optional extra that supplements the elevated attributes of intellectual capacity and objective reasoning. However, this line of thought has been challenged as Zennials have added their voice to conversations that have been culturally muted for decades. The trend of increasing use of counsellors and mental health services shows that the stigma towards mental health has lessened. Being more aware of and accepting of mental health concerns in general will hopefully lead to more open discussion about psychological problems and how to manage stress and emotions in the workplace.

This new openness that recognizes that human beings are not merely manikins employed to fulfil a role compliantly, without questioning preconceived notions and ideals, allows emotional and spiritual longing for fulfilment to be brought front and centre. A new generation has the opportunity to redefine and re-establish social norms that embody the entirety of a purpose, with a holistic view about what a person's wellbeing entails. However, this is not merely an opportunity for counsellors to line their pockets, or for society to facilitate and enable learned helplessness across industries and spheres of influence – it is an invitation to build a much-needed resilience in a generation that will have to face complexities and uncertainties that previous generations did not face. And on this foundation the new socially energized capitalism will be built.

With access to the entire world in our pockets and new relationships just one swipe away, levels of anxiety and layers of complexity are going to permeate every aspect of society at deeper degrees and greater dimensions than ever before. Painting over a lack of fulfilment due to a lack of purpose will be easy to do short term but is not sustainable long term. A shift to a greater openness to what Boomers would regard as soft issues must be embraced, and previous perspectives perhaps eliminated from social discourse. This will continue to have a measurable effect on the way in which Zennials choose to work, and on how they will invest their time, their energy and their money.

Part of the resistance to openly engaging in areas of vulnerability and authenticity for the Boomer generation lies in a deep scepticism about how this openness to non-rigorous, non-rational behaviour will lead to a dislocation in capital markets. Adopting this view misses the Zennial desire for a complete, holistic experience of human life that is not an alternative to rational analysis but a complementary activity that factors in the emotional and spiritual needs that could enhance every activity they are involved with. Equipping this generation with the necessary tools to build resilience and to bolster their mental resources can only bring benefits to businesses, companies and organizations that need to rely on individuals to make sound financial judgements under pressure – individuals who embody consistency, and enhance profit margins, while actively living with purpose.

REPAIRING BROKEN BONDS

It is my view that during the Global Financial Crisis, the single most important failure occurred in the belief that human beings could be atomized into discrete operating silos. The executives during the week were assumed to be the hard-working, grinding-away cog, and only at the weekend did they become the parent dealing with family matters and becoming human to the children in their care. This lack of integration eroded the possibility of integrity and divided up the human person, as it created a distinction between the person and the function they fulfilled at work. A person's financial judgements relating to risk, the restraints of greed, and the assumption that due to a lack of regulation they could not fail, were separated from the values and ethical stances a person could express outside the four walls of the office.

I believe our purposes in life are fulfilled when we recognize that in the workplaces, the basis of the capitalist economy, we are not merely financial operators, but financial, moral and ethical beings who have a work role but also a moral responsibility. This tripartite, three-legged stool of human integration failed when it tried to settle on one spindle – that of financial judgement in the Global Financial Crisis. In this way, the Boomer generation failed the Zennials and broke the bonds of trust that is the basis of all-purposeful living. Relationships between generations will always develop at the speed of trust.

With this in mind, the future for capitalism is very encouraging as long as we acknowledge the fragility of a capitalistic system. One that is not only undergirded by public regulations controlling the financial sector, but also by a robust moral autoregulation in the industry as a whole. Here the restlessness of the Zennial generation can work positively in preventing the older generation and the political machine from overregulating the new and the entrepreneurial emerging structures.

If CO-purposing releases the grip of sceptical cynicism and makes space for future generations to exhale its reflections as they seek a holistic experience of life, the basis of fear will decrease, and the entire ecosystem will not collapse.

Imagining a world where there is sound financial judgement, ethical considerations expressed, and emotional satisfaction as a holistic experience to be fully satisfied is not an alternative substitute to rational analysis. It is in fact a complementary supplement that nurtures the emotional and spiritual needs that are the building blocks to sustainable progress in the workplace. Spirituality is the recognition of this integrated mode of operation, and the rejection of a one-dimensional sphere that is confined to purely analytical finance.

Through this integration there will be energized and intergenerational groups of people exploring, analysing, encouraging, coaching and correcting each other. This mutual reciprocity is imperative if the capitalist system – which has been the underpinning of the freedom of the Western world – is to continue.

It appears that a new generation, while dismissing the presuppositions of a previous one, is wanting to build a community that is both genuine and authentic. And one that will incorporate not merely the rationalist basis of a previous one, but the building of CO on the basis of reason, justice and freedom. The framework this generation has sought to develop has not produced the community that they aspire to create and be a part of.

What is so significant is that there is a desire to add a spiritual dimension in the search for community. A role the Church in previous generations used to fulfil.

The next generation wishes to shape an entirely integrated worldview that has a different community at its heart. Yet it lacks the ideals and transcendent experience that the Church would provide. A community that would seek to integrate purpose and profit. That draws together the economic advantages in terms of incentives. A freedom to create profit in a value-added economy but one that has a social energy that can only be realized or unleashed in a community. This longing is an existential hole that artificial intelligence is unable to fulfil.

This socially energized objective needs to be established if we are to see partnerships flourish in a world that has shown change is inevitable, not an optional extra.

We should be encouraged and energized by seeking to establish this new paradigm that wants to escape from the brokenness we see around us. CO-purpose reimagines the future and facilitates a renewed, hope-filled humanity, as each generation affirms the goodness of what it has experienced, while embracing the ways in which we can learn and work together in creating a new reality that was scarcely imaginable several decades ago.

For both our world and our businesses, being able to combine the drive, creativity and social-mindedness of today's youth, with the broad range of skills and experience of those that came before them, will mean the difference between surviving and prospering.

THE NON-NEGOTIABLE

Intergenerational collaboration is the key to saving capitalism. There is one serious health warning. Throughout the world there is a sense in which the cohort of the next generation has come to accept that the strategic advantages of a growing, state-controlled or heavily state-influenced economy is the most desirable outcome for the next phase of capitalism. This return to the big state is alarming and comes at the price of incompetent management and corrupt dealings, as the recent pandemic has shown in practically every country. It is therefore incumbent on the Boomer generation to persuade the Zennials that liberty is at stake.

And the price of liberty is constant vigilance. The blurred objectives of government cannot bring about the changes that capitalism needs. It is true that, at one end, the self-interested objectives of the market economy can be persuaded into the common good. But it is far better for this to happen from a dynamic, incentive- and value-driven base than to be taken care of by the state. This leaning towards the state, which seems to have taken hold of the imagination of a more idealistic cohort, needs to be tempered. It is a salutary reminder that authority is on loan to central government from the people, by the people and for the people.

Given the mutual challenges we face in our society, now is an imperative time for a robust debate to take place within the generations on the future role of the state and its tentacles in the market economy. Avoiding the destruction of the incentive-based market economy is the primary aim, for capitalism is the one system that is flexible enough to respond effectively to the changes that necessarily need to be made. It is a system that creates value, enshrines freedom, allows for choice and is geared towards personal and community-based philanthropy. These are freedoms that, I believe, are the central preserve of a democratic but accountable government, in which the authority loaned to them is recognized as being a payable, not an entrenched right.

Before it is too late, we need to be constantly reminding each other that the price that was paid for liberty in a previous generation should be recognized. And notwithstanding the strong desire of a generation to prosper, the common good cannot do so at the cost of freedom. This is an intergenerational dialectic that has its greatest strength in the recognition that CO, the combined forces of the generations, will ensure a prosperous and sustainable future.

Socially energized capitalism driven by the Zennials but CO-influenced by the Boomer generation will change the face of humanity.

Now, more than ever, being aware of each other's needs, challenges, viewpoints, strengths, weaknesses and perspectives – even fears – is key to unlocking the power of intergenerational collaboration, and unleashing a hope-filled CO-destiny into the world. The Clash of Generations will give way to the CO of Generations. And on this rock we will build a renewed, invigorated, sustainable, *socially energized capital* system leading to unimaginable prosperity and productivity for the benefit of the whole of humankind.

NOTES

INTRODUCTION

1 www.cerulli.com/press-releases/cerulli-anticipates-84-tril-lion-in-wealth-transfers-through-2045.

2 www.barclays.co.uk/smart-investor/news-and-research/mar-ket-analysis/are-you-ready-for-the-great-wealth-transfer/#ref1.

3 www.thetimes.co.uk/article/how-house-prices-made-brit-ain-an-inheritocracy-75gl7mnfv.

4 www.allianz-trade.com/en_global/news-insights/economic-in-sights/the-world-is-moving-east-fast.html.

5 Ibid.

6 www.unfpa.org/sites/default/files/pub-pdf/EN-SWOP14-Report _FINAL-web.pdf.

7 www.hsbc.com/insight/topics/seven-steps-to-tackle-a-usd50-tril-lion-challenge.

8 eciu.net/analysis/briefings/net-zero/net-zero-economy-and-jobs#:~ :text=A%20net%20zero%20economy&text=Economies%20 do%20not%20stand%20still,the%20economy%20will%20be %20reduced.

9 www.cnbc.com/2022/05/03/money-decisions-by-women-will -shape-the-future-for-the-united-states.html#:~:text=Today%2C %20women%20control%20more%20than,the%20end%20of %20the%20decade.

10 www.mckinsey.com/industries/financial-services/our-insights/ women-as-the-next-wave-of-growth-in-us-wealth-management.

11 www.thetimes.co.uk/article/we-are-a-nation-divided-as-never-be-fore-by-age-5j50d9qpt.

12 www.statista.com/statistics/367796/uk-median-age-by-region/.

13 www.thetimes.co.uk/article/we-are-a-nation-divided-as-never-be-fore-by-age-5j50d9qpt.

14 www.bbc.co.uk/news/uk-63857329.

1 THE GENERATION GAME

1 www.forbes.com/sites/chriswestfall/2022/01/19/no-one-wants-to
-workthe-why-behind-the-great-resignation/?sh=748c3c0b72d7.
2 twitter.com/paulisci/status/1549527748950892544.
3 investors.fiverr.com/press-releases/press-releases-details/2022/Fiverr-
Announces-Fourth-Quarter-and-Full-Year-2021-Results/default.aspx.
4 *Time*, February 2020.
5 theconversation.com/london-2012-olympics-how-it-boosted
-medal-winning-but-failed-to-inspire-a-generation-187383.
6 www-jstor-org.lonlib.idm.oclc.org/stable/pdf/591659.pdf.
7 www.theatlantic.com/family/archive/2021/10/millennials-gen-z-
boomers-generations-are-fake/620390/.
8 http://www.stat.columbia.edu/~gelman/research/unpublished/co-
hort_voting_20191017.pdf.
9 *Time*, February 2022, p. 44.
10 eu.usatoday.com/story/money/2020/06/12/how-many-people
-were-born-the-year-you-were-born/111928356/.
11 app.ft.com/content/cbc246ee-202b-4b3f-b547-dd3533da5611
?sectionid=lunch-with-the-ft.
12 Paul Volcker, the Federal Reserve chair from 1979 to 1987 who
was credited with ending high levels of inflation.
13 www.entrepreneur.com/money-finance/3-ways-to-prepare-your-
self-for-the-great-wealth-transfer/434715.
14 thetimes.co.uk/article/cancel-culture-young-people-aren-t-intoler
ant-olivia-petter-pxwb6536s.
15 Ibid.
16 www.brookings.edu/research/lessons-from-the-end-of-free-col-
lege-in-england/.
17 www.cfr.org/backgrounder/us-student-loan-debt-trends-economic
-impact.
18 www.globest.com/2022/04/26/the-share-of-millennials-owning
-homes-is-dwindling/?slreturn=20220921105702.
19 www.thetimes.co.uk/article/we-are-a-nation-divided-as-never-be-
fore-by-age-5j50d9qpt.
20 www.generationrent.org/about_renting.
21 www.theguardian.com/money/2022/aug/06/quiet-quitting-why
-doing-the-bare-minimum-at-work-has-gone-global.
22 www.gallup.com/workplace/349484/state-of-the-global-work-
place-2022-report.aspx.

23 www.thetimes.co.uk/article/how-america-is-alienating-us-from
   -europe-r3g6xgcm6?shareToken=4780e4f3f8b61c8edb7e9e8
   4472677b0.
24 Ibid.
25 www.nytimes.com/2022/10/21/world/europe/marlene-engelhorn
   -wealth-tax.html.
26 Ibid.
27 Ibid.

2 THE CRISIS IN CAPITALISM

1 unherd.com/2022/07/how-we-became-the-dropout-society/.
2 *Sapiens*, p. 275.
3 www.independent.co.uk/news/science/apollo-11-moon-landing
   -mobile-phones-smartphone-iphone-a8988351.html.
4 www.cityam.com/worlds-smes-will-need-as-much-as-50-trillion
   -to-make-net-zero-says-hsbc-and-bcg-report.
5 www.wsj.com/articles/melvin-plotkin-gamestop-losses-memes-
   tock-11643381321.
6 twitter.com/MattBallen4791/status/1591319274307850241?s
   =20&t=OgQWVoe413GfoUtUBNrGKw.
7 www.coingecko.com/en/global-charts#:~:text=The%20global
   %20cryptocurrency%20market%20cap,a%20Bitcoin%20domi-
   nance%20of%2036.91%25.
8 www.forbes.com/sites/stevenehrlich/2022/12/13/exclusive-tran-
   script-the-full-testimony-sbf-planned-to-give-to-congress/?sh
   =456a68223c47.
9 edition.cnn.com/audio/podcasts/one-thing/episodes/312ab652
   -ed99-407d-8768-af6d0141cdfb.
10 nymag.com/intelligencer/article/sam-bankman-fried-ftx-bank-
   ruptcy-what-happened.html.
11 www.stilt.com/blog/2021/03/vast-majority-crypto-buyers-millen-
   nials-gen-z/.
12 www.cnbc.com/2022/11/11/ftx-ceo-sam-bankman-fried-lost-bil-
   lionaire-status-filed-bankruptcy.html.
13 www.reuters.com/technology/goldman-sachs-hunt-bargain-cryp-
   to-firms-after-ftx-fiasco-2022-12-06/.
14 www.spectator.co.uk/article/like-it-or-not-cryptocurrency-is-here
   -to-stay.
15 Ibid.

16 tech.eu/2022/07/25/despite-market-worries-peter-thiel-backed
    -shares-nabs-40-million-for-its-social-investing-app/.
17 Ibid.
18 www.ftadviser.com/regulation/2022/11/21/fca-warns-against
    -gamification/.
19 time.com/6095560/china-common-prosperity/.
20 www.reuters.com/world/china/chinas-push-common-prosperity
    -does-not-mean-killing-rich-official-2021-08-26/.
21 www.lse.ac.uk/ideas/Assets/Documents/updates/LSEIdeas-Decod-
    ing-Chinas-Common-Prosperity-Drive.pdf.
22 www.quantinuum.com/about.
23 crypto.com/research/2021-crypto-market-sizing-report-2022
    -forecast.

3 THE TECH FISSURE

1 www.marcprensky.com/writing/Prensky%20-%20Digital%20
   Natives,%20Digital%20Immigrants%20-%20Part1.pdf.
2 www.youtube.com/watch?v=EuWUjLocHrI.
3 millennialjournal.com/2020/10/05/pope-francis-on-the-problem
   -with-social-media-and-digital-relationships/.

4 THE CHALLENGE OF INDIVIDUALISM

1 www.highsnobiety.com/p/social-media-narcissism/.
2 www.vogue.com.au/culture/features/admit-it-you-love-yourself
   -when-did-we-become-so-selfobsessed/news-story/7a199fa21a1
   72ecd0579d55534413f58.
3 www.mentalhealth.org.uk/our-work/public-engagement/unlock
   -loneliness/loneliness-young-people-research-briefing.
4 quarterly.gospelinlife.com/a-biblical-critique-of-secular-justice
   -and-critical-theory/.

5 THE END OF TRUTH

1 www.the-tls.co.uk/articles/cynical-theories-helen-pluckrose-james
   -lindsay-book-review/.
2 unherd.com/thepost/kathleen-stock-wins-free-speech-debate-at
   -cambridge/.
3 www2.deloitte.com/content/dam/Deloitte/es/Documents/human
   -capital/Deloitte-ES-HC-Millennial-Survey-2019.pdf.

4 www.edelman.com/trust/2022-trust-barometer?utm_source=sub-stack&utm_medium=email.
5 www.the-tls.co.uk/articles/cynical-theories-helen-pluckrose-james-lindsay-book-review/.

6 UNDERSTANDING CO

1 www.thetimes.co.uk/article/the-young-are-in-desperate-need-of-optimism-btwf0kj2t.

7 CO-LEADING

1 www.edelman.com/sites/g/files/aatuss191/files/2022-01/Trust%2022_Top10.pdf.
2 www.eff.org/cyberspace-independence.
3 Foroohar, R., *Don't Be Evil*, p. 3.
4 www.theguardian.com/society/2019/dec/17/decade-of-perpetual-crisis-2010s-disrupted-everything-but-resolved-nothing.
5 www.theatlantic.com/ideas/archive/2020/08/22-year-old-blogger-behind-protests-belarus/615526/?

8 CO-WORKING

1 wiki.coworking.org/w/page/35382594/Coworking%20Manifes-to%20%28global%20-%20for%20the%20world%29.
2 www.ncci.com/SecureDocuments/QEB/QEB_Q4_2020_Remote-Work.html.
3 www.ons.gov.uk/employmentandlabourmarket/peopleinwork/employmentandemployeetypes/articles/ishybridworkingheretostay/2022-05-23#:~:text=More%20than%20three%2Dquarters%20(78,had%20fewer%20distractions%20(53%25).
4 www.thetimes.co.uk/article/work-from-home-trend-has-peaked-linkedin-survey-finds-8s5jv70bq.
5 www.bbc.co.uk/news/business-62908411.
6 Ibid.
7 www.weforum.org/agenda/2022/06/the-great-resignation-is-not-over/.
8 www.forbes.com/sites/davidsturt/2016/01/13/true-or-false-employees-today-only-stay-one-or-two-years/?sh=43a1f0c6b4c7.
9 fii-institute.org/conference/fii-6/.

10 www.archbishopofcanterbury.org/priorities/reconciliation/difference-course.
11 hbr.org/2021/03/are-you-really-listening.
12 www.theatlantic.com/education/archive/2019/02/the-explosion-of-women-teachers/582622/.
13 www.ethnicity-facts-figures.service.gov.uk/workforce-and-business/workforce-diversity/school-teacher-workforce/latest.
14 www.buffalo.edu/catt/develop/theory/constructivism.html.
15 edtheory.blogspot.com/2019/11/generational-differences-and-its-impact.html.
16 www.purewow.com/family/gen-x-characteristics.

9 CO-COMPASSION

1 www.thetimes.co.uk/article/christian-beliefs-have-lost-their-social-cachet-w59n6lgd5.

10 CO-CREATING

1 www.forbes.com/sites/benjaminlaker/2022/07/12/co-creation-a-powerful-tool-for-organizations-looking-to-become-more-innovative/?sh=6cd083e4579d.
2 Ibid.
3 www.mckinsey.com/capabilities/people-and-organizational-performance/our-insights/the-search-for-purpose-at-work.
4 www.bcorporation.net/en-us/movement.
5 fortune.com/fortune500/.
6 www.nytimes.com/2021/06/09/business/exxon-mobil-engine-no1-activist.html.
7 www.wsj.com/articles/the-hedge-fund-manager-who-did-battle-with-exxonand-won-11623470420.
8 www.unily.com/insights/blogs/unily-and-yougov-find-employees-could-hold-the-key-to-a-strong-comeback-from-covid-19.

CONCLUSION

1 news.sky.com/story/why-its-more-difficult-for-young-people-to-buy-a-house-now-than-it-was-fifty-years-ago-12537254
2 www.mckinsey.com/capabilities/people-and-organizational-performance/our-insights/the-great-attrition-is-making-hiring-harder-are-you-searching-the-right-talent-pools.

INDEX